Sea Fishing

Other titles in the Crowood Fishing Facts series:

River Trout Fishing   Pat O'Reilly
Stillwater Trout Fishing   Chris Ogborne
Fly Tying   Pat O'Reilly
Pike Fishing   Tony Miles
Carp Fishing   Tony Miles

FISHING FACTS

SEA FISHING

EXPERT ADVICE FOR BEGINNERS

TREVOR HOUSBY

Illustrations by Paul Martin

The Crowood Press

First published in 1991 by
The Crowood Press Ltd
Ramsbury, Marlborough
Wiltshire SN8 2HR

British Library Cataloguing in Publication Data

Housby, Trevor, 1939–
Sea fishing. – (Fishing facts series)
1. Fishing (Field sports)
I. Title
799.16

ISBN 1 85223 473 3

Dedication
To my son Russell, who loves the sea
as much as I do. Long may he fish.

Typeset by PCS Typesetting, Frome, Somerset.
Printed and bound in Great Britain by
BPCC Hazell Books, Aylesbury

Contents

Introduction

In recent years sea angling has become an increasingly popular sport. This book then is designed to give a basic all-round view of sea fishing tackle and techniques. Hopefully, it will hold appeal for both the novice and the more experienced angler alike.

There was a time when sea fishing was a rough and ready sport. However, today's anglers are more sophisticated. Tackle and techniques have improved beyond all recognition, so much so that an angler can now specialize in catching whichever species he finds most appealing.

Modern materials have made tackle production an art. The days when reels were made of steel and plastic are long gone and both rods and reels are light enough to handle all day. Today reels are made of titanium, giving lightness and strength without making them heavy to use. The same applies to beach and boat rods, most of which are made of a carbon–glass mix, which combines maximum strength with minimum weight.

It's up to the angler to decide which branch of sea angling he wishes to participate in. Often his interests may overlap, so that the year is made up of shore and boat fishing trips. For many, the appeal of shore fishing lies in the fact that apart from petrol and bait money, the fishing is free. The boat angler, on the other hand, may have to pay ten to twenty pounds for his place on a boat. This outlay, however, is normally covered by an increase in catch. Most sea fish are edible, and a few plump plaice and a hefty cod or two can make a welcome addition to the family table.

This book will hopefully help to iron out the pitfalls that beset many newcomers to sea fishing and semi-experienced anglers. Far too many anglers go out full of enthusiasm and end up purchasing equipment which is totally wrong for their intended fishing area. To try to avoid money wastage of this kind, it is a good idea to join a recommended sea angling club. There are thousands of such clubs in Britain and many, surprisingly enough, are situated in inland towns. Once a club has been joined, its members will be quick to point the newcomer in the right direction. Most of these clubs run regular trips to specific areas. Their members know to the last detail what is needed to fish their chosen venues and tackle can be purchased accordingly.

Some anglers may only indulge in sea fishing during holiday time, the rest of the year being spent coarse fishing. Obviously, these people don't want to splash out on expensive equipment. In

INTRODUCTION

many instances their existing tackle can be adequate. A glass or cane rod can be used to float fish for mackerel or garfish, or for light bottom fishing for flounders, or to tackle mullet.

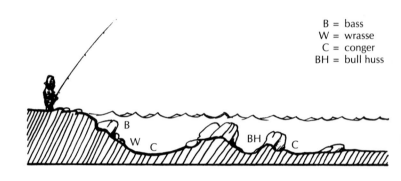

B = bass
W = wrasse
C = conger
BH = bull huss

The only thing to remember is to wash and oil tackle after use. Sea water can be corrosive; reels, reel fittings and rod rings must therefore be thoroughly cleaned after each session. To ensure a long life, tackle should always be maintained. Fortunately, most sea anglers enjoy tinkering with tackle almost as much as undertaking the fishing itself. Look after your gear well and it will repay you with years of faithful service.

There are many additions and facets to sea angling that newcomers only realize once they have been fishing for a while. Bait collecting, for example, can be particularly interesting. Any angler living close to the coastline can cut costs by digging his own ragworm or lugworm, or by collecting his own supply of crabs. Bait collecting in itself can become a hobby, but it is essential to set about it correctly. Many anglers, for example, excavate holes and trenches for worms, then neglect to fill them in before leaving the beach. Once the tide covers such a hole, a paddling child can easily step into it with possible fatal effect.

Introduction

Crab collecting poses a similar problem. A crab in the process of shedding its shell will take cover under a weed-covered rock or similar obstacle. The same rock may also give cover to a host of other sea creatures. If you turn over a rock to take a crab, make certain you turn it back before moving the next stone. In this way you will not create havoc with other forms of marine life.

Sea fishing is a fascinating sport which, once taken up, should give a new perspective to angling.

SEA FISH SPECIES

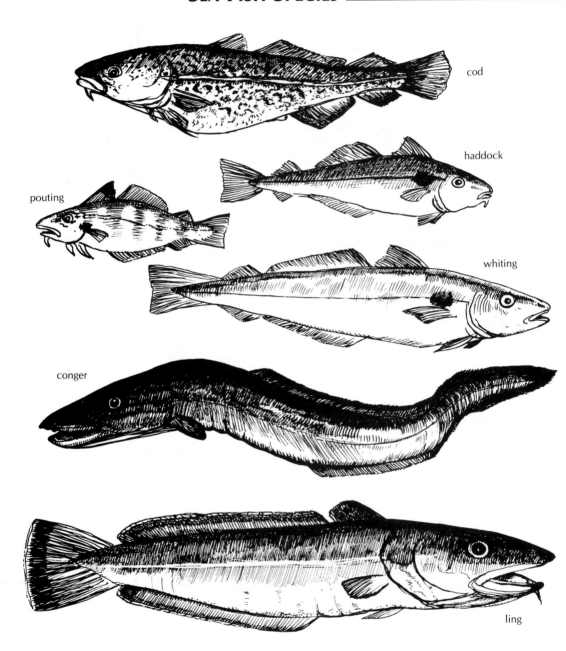

cod

haddock

pouting

whiting

conger

ling

Sea Fish Species

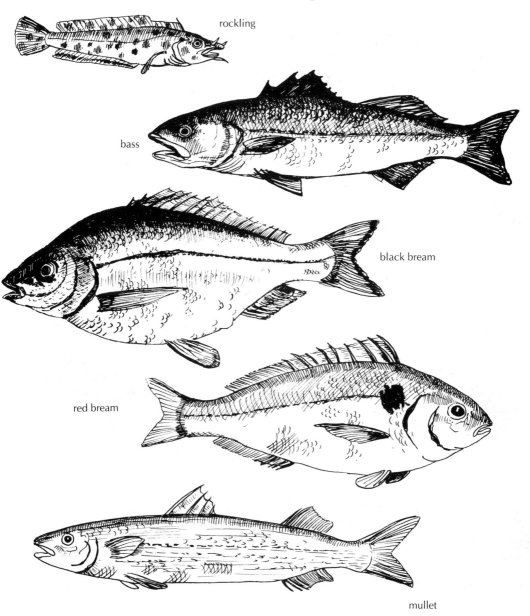

rockling

bass

black bream

red bream

mullet

Sea Fish Species ——————————

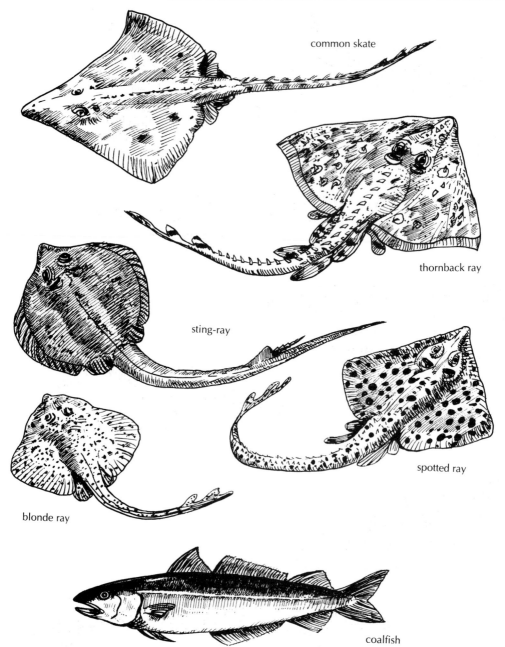

common skate

thornback ray

sting-ray

spotted ray

blonde ray

coalfish

Sea Fish Species

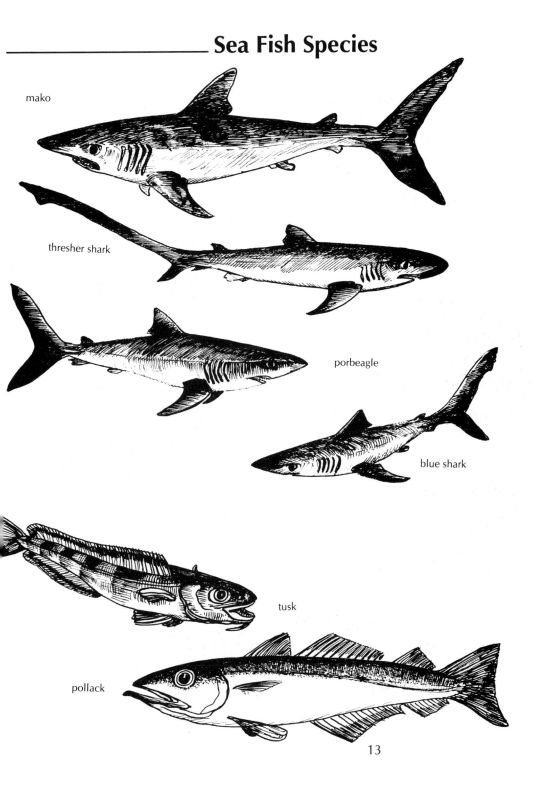

mako

thresher shark

porbeagle

blue shark

tusk

pollack

SEA FISH SPECIES

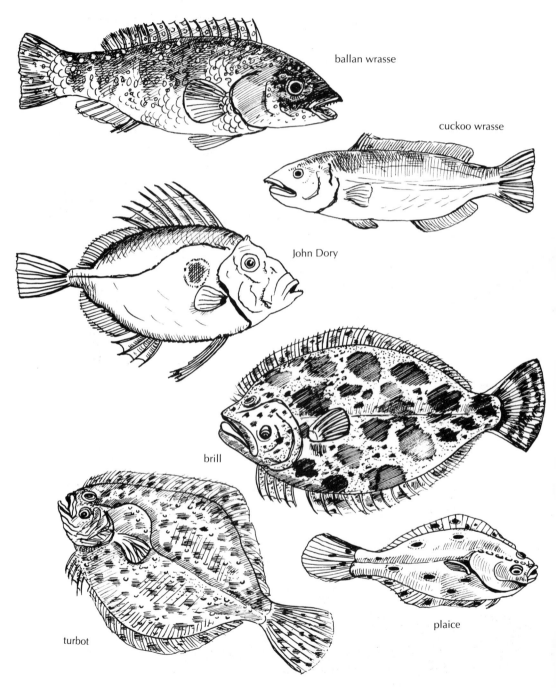

ballan wrasse

cuckoo wrasse

John Dory

brill

turbot

plaice

Sea Fish Species

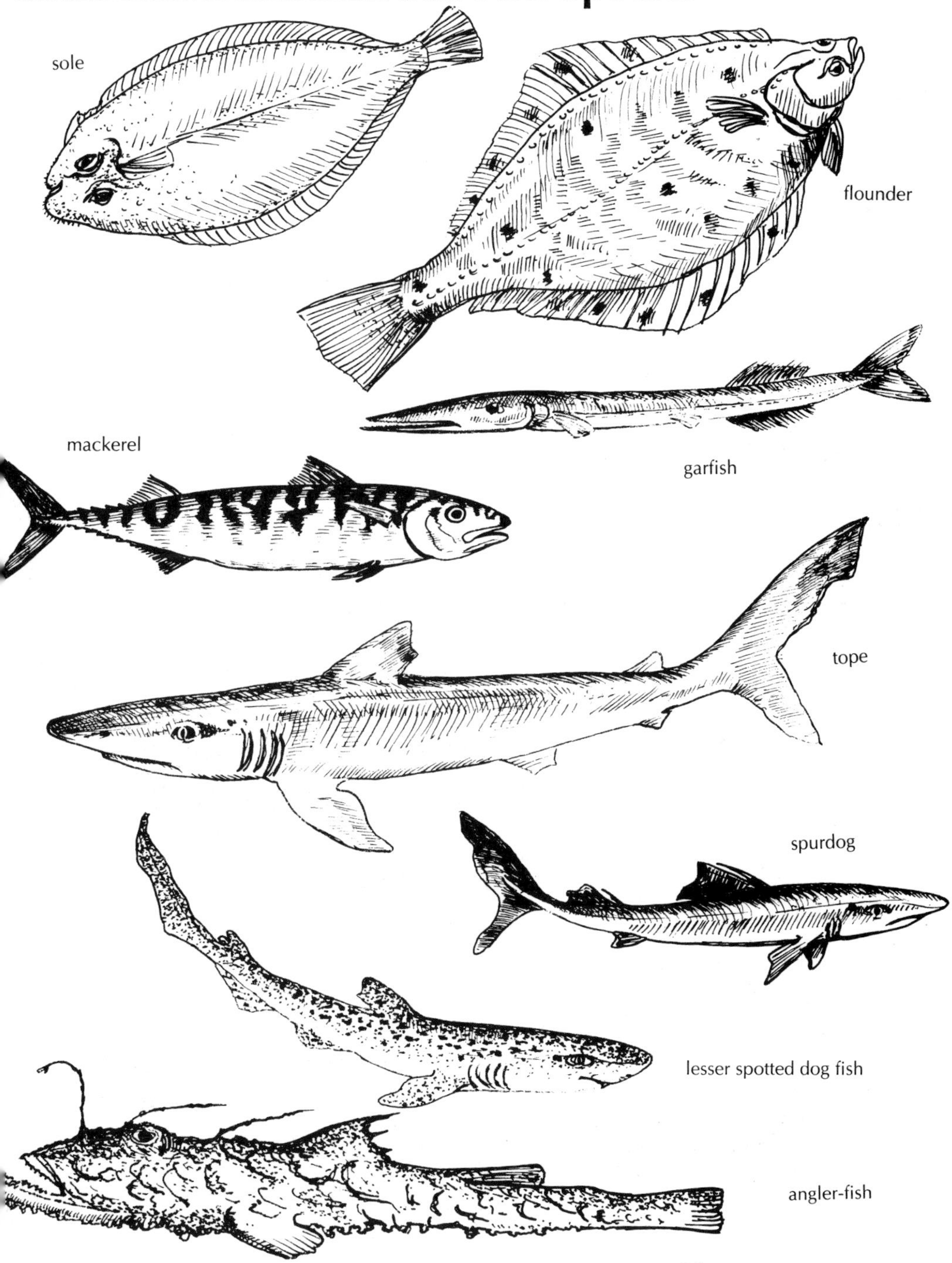

sole

flounder

garfish

mackerel

tope

spurdog

lesser spotted dog fish

angler-fish

15

PERSONAL SAFETY

Every year anglers are involved in serious accidents, most of them usually ending in fatalities. Most of these accidents are caused by not thinking or going against sound advice. Many anglers are either swept out to sea during rough seas or because of rising tides, or drown in small boat accidents.

Advice to Boat Anglers

Invariably, the victims of boat accidents have set out with bad weather imminent. Make no mistake, the sea on a good day may look calm and inviting but can change within seconds into a raging killer. Respect the sea and it will respect you. Never take chances with it. If the weather forecast is 'iffy', stay home – you can always go fishing another time. Small boat or dinghy anglers should also carry and wear a life-jacket. If you do end up in the sea that jacket could save your life. Never overload a small boat with people. This is easily done, but when the weather changes, too many guests can become a nightmare.

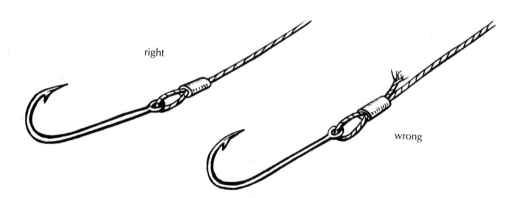

right

wrong

Correct crimping will prevent tail fraying and any nasty cuts.

Finally, a warning on crimping wire traces for big fish. Many anglers leave a projecting tail of wire, the idea being that this gives the crimp a chance to slip without losing a hooked fish. In theory this is good, but in practice it is dangerous. Exposed wire

16

will fray and if your hand comes into contact with it, the resulting wounds can be deep and painful. Never leave any projecting wire; instead, make sure that the tail of wire is cut so the crimp amply covers it. In this way you may save yourself a nasty injury.

Advice to Rock Anglers

Rock anglers also put themselves unnecessarily in danger. Their first mistakes are to not say where they intend to fish and to not tell anyone when to expect them back. Rock marks often entail a cliff scramble or a long hike through rough terrain. A fall in these situations can lead to a severe sprain or broken bones. Either way, it is impossible to walk and unless you have a friend who can go

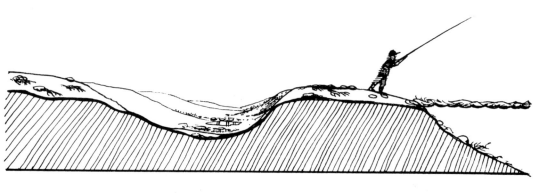

for help or somebody who will know if you fail to return, you could be in serious trouble – not so bad if you happen to be above the high-tide mark but potentially lethal if you are below it. A rock mark safe at low water could turn into a death-trap as the tide starts to rise. Remember if you cross a dry gully on the way out to your fishing station to keep an eye on the rising tide. What may appear to be a harmless shallow depression when empty can become quite treacherous when the sea comes creeping back. Tides therefore have to be watched constantly as well as heavy seas that break on the rocks from which you normally fish.

Look behind; the gully can fill when the tide floods.

Beach Fishing

Britain is surrounded by beaches, most of which provide some sort of fishing potential. Some beaches are summer venues. Others come on song when the first winter frosts cause water temperatures to drop. For many anglers beach fishing is a regular pastime. Most beaches are open to the public and once you have purchased the right tackle, beach angling becomes an inexpensive form of fishing.

Getting Started

Before you even attempt to purchase any tackle you must first decide where you intend to do most of your fishing. Having decided on locality it is then essential to spend time there, so that you can watch local anglers fishing. By talking to them you will get a lot of sensible advice on your ultimate choice of tackle.

Many beaches are used regularly for competition fishing, often attended by top beach fishermen. These competitions are also worthwhile attending as a spectator. Competition anglers are usually experienced with some good tips to offer to the novice. However, remember each competitor is there with the motivation to win. Never attempt to talk to competition anglers while a contest is in progress.

Once you have an idea of your requirements, go to a recommended tackle shop in the area of your proposed fishing grounds where you can speak to the staff and ask their advice. By this time you should be able to make your purchase with confidence.

Never buy important tackle from a dealer far away. You may make a costly investment and find that it does not suit the coastline where you intend to fish. Many anglers have made this expensive mistake when it is already too late to exchange the tackle for the correct gear.

Terminal Tackle

Beach tackle should be kept as simple as possible. For cod, whiting and species off the bottom a one- or two-hook nylon paternoster gives a perfect bait presentation. For flat-fish, ray,

18

conger and spurdog a plain running ledger rig is ideal. There are many variations on these basic themes, but these two rigs make a good starting point. As your angling expertise increases, your terminal tackle can become more technical. Take your venture step by step – you will then be unlikely to go wrong.

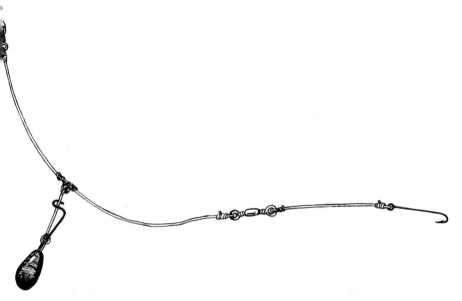

A simple ledger rig.

Newcomers to beach fishing often make the mistake of thinking that all beaches are of similar layout. This is far from true. If you visit a given beach on a low-water spring tide you will be able to see that the bottom contours vary considerably. More importantly still, you will be able to see and map obstructions and gullies that are important to fish location. Understanding a beach layout is as important as purchasing the right tackle. It is therefore necessary to look at some basic beaches and see how they differ and the sort of fish they may produce.

Surf Beaches

A true surf beach is normally shallow and totally exposed to prevailing winds. The best surf beaches are situated on the

BEACH FISHING

Cornish peninsula and along the west coasts of Wales and Ireland. Such beaches normally are best for fishing just after a 'blow'. Heavy onshore winds stir up sand and gravel and dig out a superabundance of different types of edible creatures. Crabs, razor fish, shrimps and sandeels all make a tasty meal for fish hunting for food.

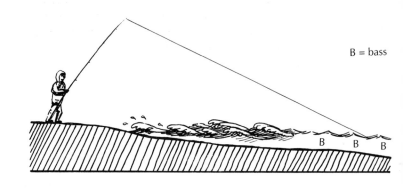

B = bass

A surf beach.

Surf beaches are normally shallow and haunted especially by bass. However, when the waters are calm flounder and the odd sole may also be present. Bass are very much a prize catch and many anglers specialize in catching these beautiful fish. A normally deserted surf beach may often become alive with angling activity during popular fishing periods. Knowledgeable bass anglers normally cast to drop their bait behind the third breaker, which may look like a maelstrom of surging water but is just what bass like. The most experienced surf-beach fishermen use medium-weight beachcasters 12 or 13ft in length for this sort of work. Such rods will handle leads of 3–6oz. The choice of reel really depends on personal preference and casting ability, but many experienced anglers prefer a multiplying reel. A good modern fixed spool like the Shimano Biomaster can make casting easy; nowadays many anglers seem to be switching to this particular reel.

Types of Beach

Steep to Shingle Beaches

A steep to shingle beach drops rapidly into deep water. Some of the finest fishing beaches in this country – Dungeness in Kent, Milford shingle bank in Hampshire and Dorset's magnificent Chesil Beach – are of this type. Fish are present on a year-round basis. Although fish species may change with each season, the fishing remains good. For example, Chesil Beach during winter can produce plenty of big cod. Cod catches are usually interspersed with whiting and bouts of large spurdog activity. However, during spring, summer and autumn catches of bass, sole, conger, tope, mackerel, garfish and recently the normally subtropical trigger-fish, are common. Thornback ray and small-eyed ray also occur.

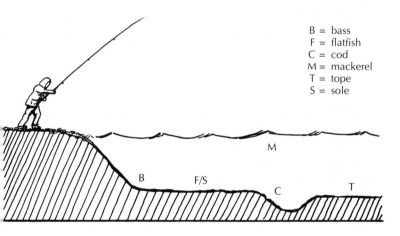

B = bass
F = flatfish
C = cod
M = mackerel
T = tope
S = sole

These beaches are often subjected to strong tidal activity. For this reason and because of the average large size of fish present, a heavy beachcaster's outfit is widely used. A rod capable of casting a 6–8oz lead is the most popular. Long casting is seldom necessary unless the bait has to be cast to a specific fish-holding

A steep to shingle beach.

21

area. Fish usually expect to find most of their food at the base of the beach drop-off. If an offshore gully can be located it may prove to be extremely productive. Even a 12in-deep trench can act as a roadway for patrolling fish. Regular anglers tend to prefer multiplying reels to fixed spool reels, which have certain limitations when hooking a big cod or good-sized conger.

Natural baits used on steep to shingle beaches tend to be larger than those used on shallower beaches. Mackerel fillets, whole sprats, calamari squid and crab are among the popular baits at Milford shingle bank and on the Chesil bank. Further east at Dungeness, worms (especially black and yellow tailed lugworms) are the real killers. Normally four to six of these worms are crammed onto a hook to make a large very edible bait loved by cod and whiting. Another successful bait used particularly when ray and conger are on the move is a fresh whole pouting or a fillet of pouting. It must be fresh, though, in order to be effective. Pouting are common along any steep to shingle beaches.

During the summer months vast shoals of mackerel may sweep along these beaches. Many anglers then switch from natural baits to strings of four or six feathers, which are cast out as far as possible and retrieved at speed. Beach mackerel are often suicidal and can be caught in huge numbers.

Rocky Beaches

In areas where the sea bed is made up of rock formations surrounded by areas of flat sand or gravel, fishing is often excellent. Species are normally limited; bass, cod and conger being the most common depending on the time of year and the locality of the beach. In the Channel Islands large plaice and black bream are also common inhabitants of rocky beaches while certain spots around Alderney Island yield fine black bream right through the winter period.

All beaches are best for fishing on a night tide, the rocky beach being no exception. The rocky beach usually calls for similar tackle and baits used in steep to shingle beach fishing. Tackle losses are normally high. To cut costs many anglers either make their own leads or attach their leads using a heavy elastic band. If a lead does become snagged, pressure can then be applied so that

Types of Beach

the band breaks and the remainder of the terminal tackle is not lost.

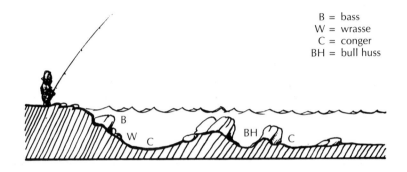

B = bass
W = wrasse
C = conger
BH = bull huss

A rocky beach.

Mud Flat Beaches

These are often shallow and comparatively featureless beaches occurring in areas like the Solent or along the Essex coast. The target species on such beaches are the ungainly sting-ray and the racy-looking smoothound, both fast-moving fish capable of making long runs. The smoothound in particular can make a spectacular dash for freedom.

Both species take worm and crab baits. Of the two species, the sting-ray is the more difficult and dangerous to handle. Solent sting-ray specialists often carry a flat length of wood. When the ray is beached, this wood is placed over the tail with the angler standing on either end while extracting the hook from the ray's mouth. The wood stops the ray from lashing its whip-like spine-armed tail around. In the old days anglers often cut the sting-ray's tail off before attempting to unhook it. This was a cruel and barbaric practice which thankfully is no longer in use.

23

ROCK FISHING

Successful rock fishing calls for a knowledge of local conditions and the preferred habitat of individual fish species. Wrasse and conger, for example, like to lurk in deep weed-grown rock gullies, normally found close to the rocks on which anglers stand. Pollack usually hold station just above weed growth, while hunting bass are more inclined to cruise in close to the surface, where they can be caught with spinners or float-fished live bait. Bass may also hunt over the exposed rock at the bottom end of a drop-off further out, where a gully slopes upward before falling away into deep water. Large wrasse, lethargic bull huss and the odd conger often may exist in comparative harmony.

In the deeper water where rocks give way to sand, small-eyed ray and lesser spotted dogfish can be found. Above them, close to the surface, mackerel and garfish may hunt for shoals of whitebait or small sandeels.

Types of fish may change from the south to the north: bass may be replaced by cod, pollack by coalfish and small-eyed ray by thornback ray. Generally, however, the picture will remain very much the same.

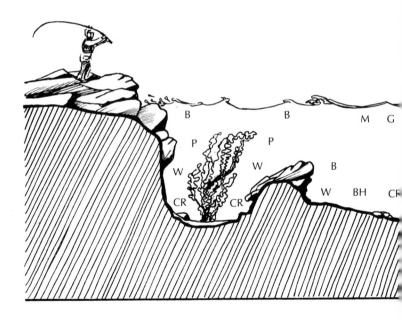

Fish location.

Fish Location

Tackle

Type of tackle will change depending on the type of fish you plan to catch. For float fishing a 9 or 10ft spinning-style rod can be employed, while for conger and big wrasse a medium or even heavy beachcaster may be essential. The medium-weight rod can also be used for longer casting for ray or lesser spotted dogfish.

A Word of Warning

Rock fishing can be dangerous and accidents can occur. Never go rock fishing alone and always tell someone where you are going to fish and what time you intend to return. Should an accident occur, the coast guard will then know just where to find you.

Always watch that the sea does not creep round behind you. A gully that is easy to cross at low tide can become treacherous at high tide. Equally important, watch out for freak waves. Many anglers are washed away each year.

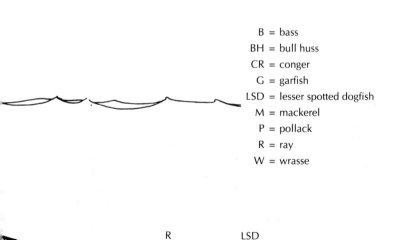

B = bass
BH = bull huss
CR = conger
G = garfish
LSD = lesser spotted dogfish
M = mackerel
P = pollack
R = ray
W = wrasse

R   LSD

sand

ROCK FISHING

Rock fish are normally active hunters used to finding their main food on or around the rocks where they live. For this reason fresh bait natural to the area is more likely to catch these fish than stale or imported bait.

Bait collecting can be just as much fun as fishing. The ideal time to collect bait is at low water when the outgoing tide has left acres of rock exposed.

Crabs

By turning over large stones you can catch many hard-backed shore crabs which make first-class wrasse bait. Crabs the size of a fifty-pence piece are the best. They can be kept alive in a plastic bait bucket half filled with damp seaweed. Plastic buckets make the best containers, as metal buckets seem to kill off live bait very quickly.

Remember, when you turn a stone over you expose many forms of sea life. When you have removed the bait you need you should turn the stone back. This helps conserve the unwanted shrimps, sea anemones, etc.

(a)

Prawns

Rock pools filled with water by the receding tide are a good place to find prawns. Alive or dead, prawns make excellent float-fishing bait for bass and wrasse. Prawns are best caught in a net and should then be transferred directly to a bait bucket filled with fresh sea water. A live prawn should be hooked lightly, passing the point of the hook under the shell of the second segment of its body. Dead prawns can be threaded directly onto the hook.

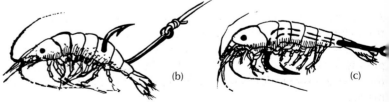

(b)

(c)

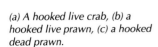
(a) A hooked live crab, (b) a hooked live prawn, (c) a hooked dead prawn.

26

Shellfish

Shellfish also make a good bait and are easily obtainable. Conical limpets are used for wrasse and should be carefully removed from rocks with a blunt thin-bladed knife. You have to be quick to insert the knife blade between the relaxed limpet shell and the rock itself. If the limpet detects your presence it will clamp itself solidly to the rock. Practice makes perfect. Once you have acquired the knack, limpet collecting becomes easy. The limpet must then be scraped from its shell. The hook should pass through the centre of the limpet so that its point just projects through the black stomach of the bait.

Northern rock fishermen use mussels in place of limpets. The flesh of a raw mussel is very soft; to prevent it falling off the hook, most anglers therefore attach it with wool or elastic thread. This is a top bait for rock cod.

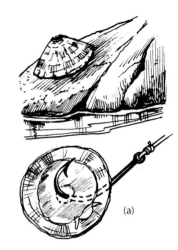

(a)

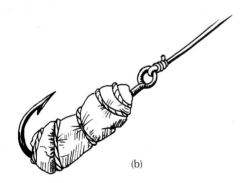

(b)

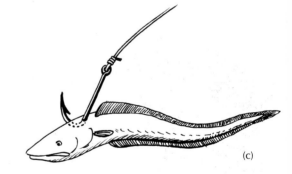

(c)

Elvers

An interesting bait is an elver or young freshwater eel. Elvers can normally be found where there is a freshwater inlet to the sea. Normally they lurk beneath flat stones. Once spotted, a lightning grab is necessary to catch them. Lightly hooked through the back they make a successful bait for pollack, coalfish, bass, garfish and mackerel.

(a) A limpet on a rock, a hooked limpet, (b) mussel flesh with wool binding, (c) an elver hooked lightly through its skin.

27

Float fishing from rocks can be a productive fun way of catching fish. To watch a float bob and jiggle before suddenly vanishing beneath the surface never fails to fascinate both the novice and the experienced angler.

As in all forms of fishing, good tackle and planning are essential.

Choice of Float

(a)   (b)

Types of float: (a) a good streamlined pattern, (b) a poor float shape that offers maximum resistance to a taking fish.

One of the commonest mistakes made by rock anglers is the wrong choice of float. Far too many anglers purchase the largest and bulkiest float they can find. Instead, a good float should be streamlined and comparatively small. A good idea is to therefore ignore all the displayed sea floats in a tackle shop and make a selection from its pike-fishing section. Pike floats make first-class sea floats, most of which look more like miniature lighthouses.

How to Use a Float

The float must be set to clear upthrust weeds on rocks.

The main purpose of any float is to support a bait at a given depth. Its use as a bite indicator is of secondary importance. Remember

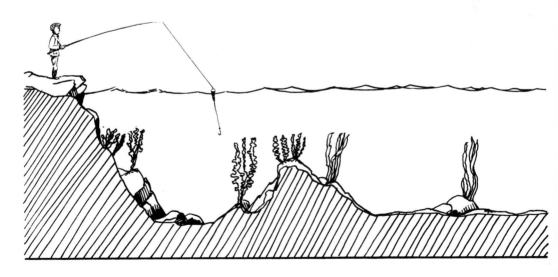

Float Fishing from Rocks

also that a float can only be set to fish over the shallowest section of a gully – any deeper and the tackle may become snagged.

Most sea floats work on the sliding principle, the depth being set by a tiny section of rubber band hitched to the line at the required distance from the hook. For example, if the water is 20ft deep and you want to fish 2ft off the sea bed, then tie the band to the line 18ft from the hook. To avoid the rubber band becoming jammed in the centre tube of the float, many anglers use a tiny shirt button or bead between it and the float top.

The majority of traces are made up of 12in of nylon with a hook at one end and a small barrel swivel on the other end. The float is slid onto the reel line as is the weight, normally a barrel type of the right size to cock the float. The trace is then tied to the end of the reel line.

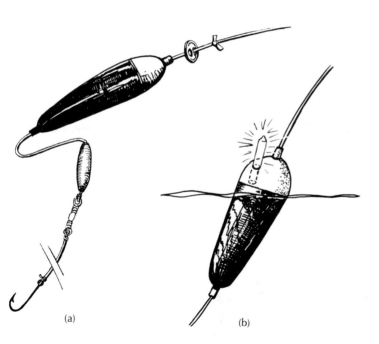

(a)   (b)

(a) A sliding float, (b) a night float.

For night fishing a 'starlight' chemical light still can be inserted into or taped to the float top. These light sticks are excellent and are stocked by most good tackle shops.

29

Pier Fishing

Since Victorian times pier fishing has been a popular part of the British sea-angling scene. Many of today's top sea anglers began their career dangling handlines from some pier. Unfortunately many of the great piers have suffered over the years, especially from increasingly strong winter winds. Despite this, pier and harbour fishing are still popular. Quite a few large fish can be caught, bringing a lot of excitement and often making news in the weekly angling papers. The unknown quantity is very much a part of the anticipation of pier fishing.

A pier or harbour arm acts in the same way as a headland. It thrusts out from the land to create a form of barrier round which fish must pass in their hunt for food. Harbour arms are of solid construction whereas a pier is built on open piles and supports. Within a few years of construction most pier supports are surrounded by healthy weed growth, which acts as a hiding place for all manner of edible creatures. Prawns, crabs and small fish all abound round pier supports and harbour walls. These in turn make a natural groundbait and food supply for resident and passing predators.

Most piers also carry cafés and restaurants from which waste

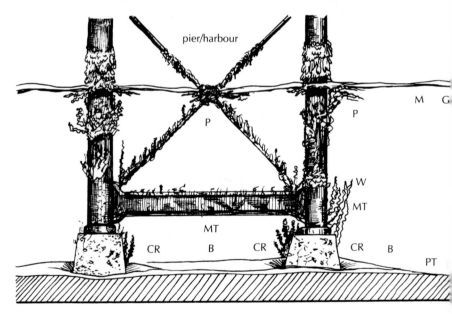

Fish location.

bread and other food find their way into the sea. These tend to attract grey mullet, and even shoaling mackerel and garfish. During the autumn harbour arms often produce excellent catches of migrating silver eels, which usually enter into the harbour via storm drains.

Know Where to Fish

The secret to pier and harbour fishing is to know where your fish are likely to be. Far too many anglers march to the end of the pier and cast out as far as possible. In most instances they overshoot the best fishing areas by many yards. The only time long casting is recommended is when the bait is cast to a specific area such as a patch of rock or an upthrust rock – the sort of place which might hold a conger or attract the attention of hunting cod. For the most part, pier fish are found under or directly in front of the pier structure or harbour stonework. Most species will be found close to the bottom. Pollack and bass might swim as high as midwater while mackerel and garfish patrol just under the surface.

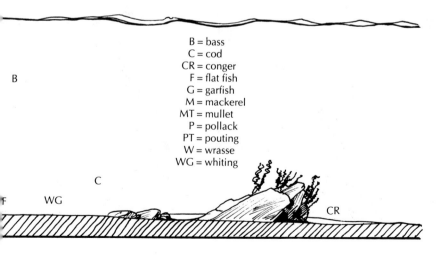

B = bass
C = cod
CR = conger
F = flat fish
G = garfish
M = mackerel
MT = mullet
P = pollack
PT = pouting
W = wrasse
WG = whiting

PIER FISHING ――――――――――

Medium-weight beachcasting tackle is near perfect for most pier and harbour fishing, while a lighter rod can be used for float or mullet fishing.

Terminal tackle used is very similar to that of rock fishing. For fish that swim from midwater to the surface a sliding float rig like the one recommended for float fishing from rocks (*see* page 00) is perfect. For the smaller bottom fish a single hook paternoster will suffice, while for larger fish a simple running ledger is ideal.

Baits

The recommended baits for catching fish which frequent pier or harbour arms are worm for wrasse, fresh pouting flesh for mullet, and fish strip for the other major species. The larger fish prefer whole or cut fish or squid.

Popular Fishing Spots

Some piers are justifiably famous for the varied catches they produce. Southend Pier is a typical example. Almost a mile in length, it is popular with both the individual and the competition angler. Favoured species are flounder, mackerel, garfish and silver eels. This pier also produces the odd bass and monster plaice. West country harbour arms produce a wide variety of fish. For example, take the lighthouse quay at Mevagissey. This produces pollack, mackerel, mullet, garfish, bass and hefty conger. There are dozens of similar venues dotted about all over England, Scotland, Ireland and Wales. All are capable of providing good safe fishing.

A Good Tip

Many anglers automatically head for the end of a pier. This is all right for catching mullet, mackerel, garfish, pollack and cod. Other species such as bass and flat-fish prefer to swim and feed closer to the shore. The middle sections of a pier are therefore often highly productive.

For bass, it pays to watch the wave patterns and take up a position that allows you to cast between the third and fourth breakers. Bass use the breakers as a natural groundbait-providing machine – worms, crabs and small fish are dug out or by the tidal action and swept out by the undertow. A good bait in this situation is peeler crab or whole or cut sandeel.

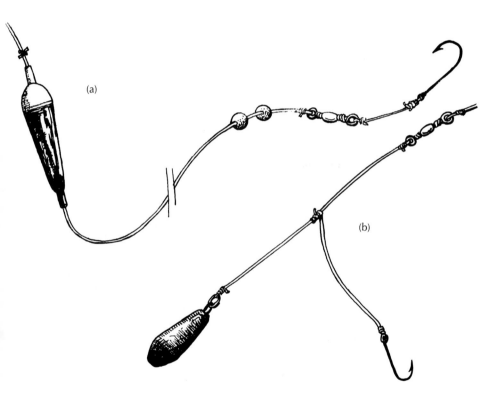

In areas where heavyweight bass are known to exist, a half mackerel or whole calamari squid can be used as bait. Remember, however: a big bait calls for a big hook.

Different rigs. (a) a float tackle, (b) a single-hook paternoster.

33

PIER FISHING

Many sea anglers regard mullet as a practically uncatchable species. This is because mullet do not conform to basic sea fish standards. They can, in fact, be caught by using the tackle and techniques of freshwater fishing rather than those of sea fishing.

The three species of grey mullet in British waters feed mostly on soft weed and its indwelling creatures. Exceptionally tackle-shy they seldom fall to a bait presented on a big hook and heavy line. Freshwater rods, 5lb BS line and size 8 or 10 freshwater-scale hooks have to be used. There are also several mullet rigs to use.

Floats or Paternosters

A freshwater float or a light nylon paternoster are the standard rigs for mullet fishing. These can be baited with fish flesh, fresh pork or beef, or bread. Regular mullet anglers use a groundbait called 'Shirvy' to attract fish. Shirvy is made up of minced fish or meat, fish or animal blood, and bran, and must be spooned sparingly into the water. Never overdo it, as too much free food will make the mullet vanish.

(a) A mullet spinner, (b) a light nylon paternoster, (c) a freshwater float.

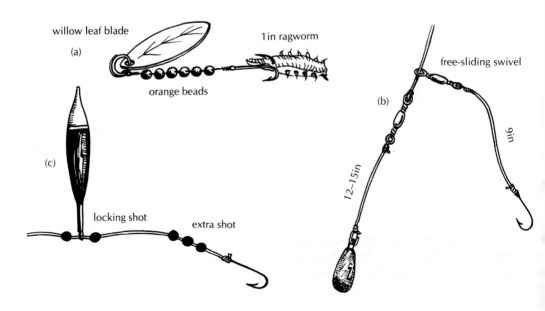

willow leaf blade

(a)

1in ragworm

free-sliding swivel

orange beads

(b)

9in

(c)

12–15in

locking shot

extra shot

34

Mullet Fishing

Anchored Crust Method for Attracting Mullet

In harbours or estuaries where mullet feed in shallow water a slice of dry bread anchored by a stone can also act as groundbait to attract and hold the shoaling fish. This, accompanied by a piece of bread on float tackle, can be deadly.

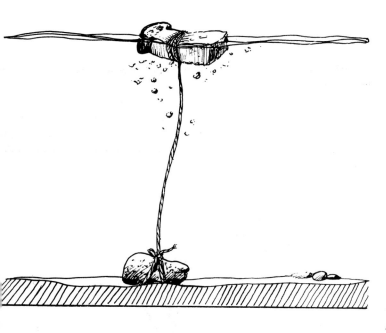

The anchored crust method for attracting mullet.

Spinners

In some estuaries the thin-lipped mullet will take a baited spinner. The spinner should be small and incorporate some orange beads in its make-up; the bait is usually a 1in section of ragworm. Once on the feed, mullet will hit this bait solidly, often hooking themselves in the process. Mullet fishing can be fun but it calls for finesse.

35

Boat Fishing

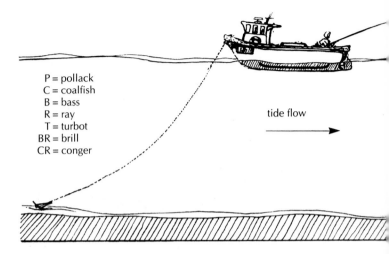

P = pollack
C = coalfish
B = bass
R = ray
T = turbot
BR = brill
CR = conger

tide flow

Fish location.

Any projecting outcrop of rocks can act as a haven for fish. These outcrops are usually charted and fished regularly. Sometimes they may be towering reefs, while at other times only a foot or two high. On the right day these reefs and rock ledges can be highly productive – provided, of course, you know when and how to fish them.

Normally, fish collect on the down-tide side of such an outcrop. This is a slack water area, where the tidal flow brings with it all manner of food items which are washed over the top of the rock to fall gently into the sheltered area behind it. To fish such a place, the boat should be anchored uptide of the rock, so that it is positioned at a point where anglers' lines can drop directly behind the projection.

Fish Location

Pollack, coalfish and bass usually swim high in the water just under the push of tide. Here they can surge out to take any small fish and sandeels that are washed past. At the base of the rock conger eels lurk; while further back but still in sheltered water, ray, turbot and brill may be found. Obviously, when the tide changes the fish move round the rock. This means that the boat has to be re-positioned.

36

Reefs or Rock Ledges

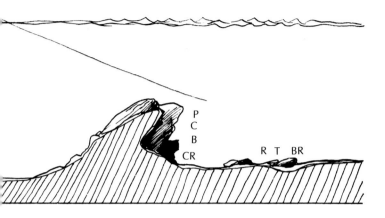

Of course, the type of fish also varies from one locality to the next. Fish common in the south may be non-existent in northern waters. For example, bass might be replaced by whiting, haddock or cod. This same area may also produce brightly coloured cuckoo wrasse or even gurnards.

Techniques

In slack-tide areas a nice way to take pollack, coalfish and bass is to use a small lead and a long flowing trace baited with ragworm, lowered down until the lead touches the rock; then the tackle should be slowly retrieved, bringing the ragworm gently upward.

Fish will often first nibble at the moving worm. When this occurs keep the bait moving upward. If you stop cranking the reel handle the attracted fish might be alarmed and vanish. The same technique can be used with a red gill or Eddystone eel. Natural baits are normally more effective than artificial ones.

For the larger bottom-dwelling species a 30 or 50 class boat rod can be used to present a large natural bait on a simple running ledger rig. In areas subjected to heavy runs of tide a wire line may be necessary to hold the terminal tackle down at fish level. Bites on this sort of gear usually follow a set pattern – a couple of hard knocks followed by a heavy pull.

Attractor Spoons

Most sea fish are attracted by movement and to a lesser extent colour. Attractor spoons manipulate both these factors and are an excellent way of catching large cod. A cod trace with a $2\frac{1}{2}$–3in plastic attractor spoon set 15in above the baited hook normally catches more than bait on its own. White and particularly coloured spoons are effective. Heavier metal spoon blades are not as good as plastic though, as they tend to sink to the bottom.

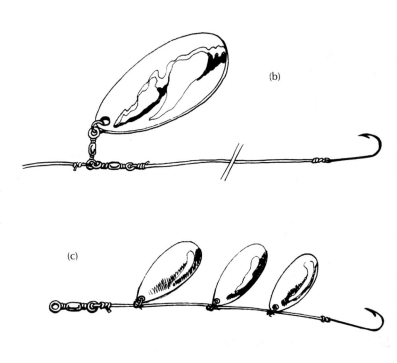

(a) Coloured beads for plaice fishing, (b) metal or plastic attractor spoon, (c) multi-spoon rig for big cod.

The vibrations of the constantly wavering spoon set up a vibration pattern that draws cod to the area of the bait. Some anglers use two or three attractor spoons on a trace, setting up a stronger vibration pattern than a single spoon blade. Attractor spoons can be fished above natural squid or worm baits.

Coloured Bead Combinations

Plaice anglers find that by adding a number of different coloured beads to a trace more fish are caught. Favoured bead combinations are red and white or red and yellow. Whether fish see this as a section of brightly coloured worm no one can tell. Used in conjunction with lugworm or ragworm, however, the beads make a significant difference to catches.

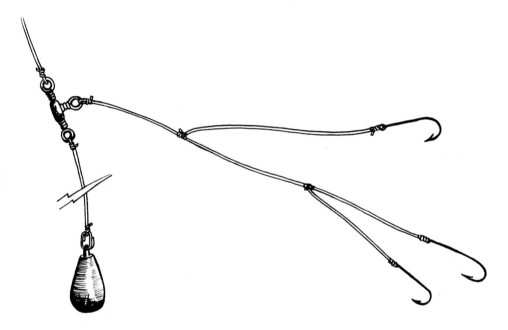

A three-hook paternoster rig.

Simple Nylon Paternoster

When small fish such as pouting, codling and whiting are on the move a simple two- or three-hook paternoster rig can be very effective. Distance between three-way swivels should be 24–30in in order to keep baits off the sea bed. This simple nylon paternoster works best in a reasonable flow of tide, where the movement of water keeps the baits fluttering temptingly above the sea bed.

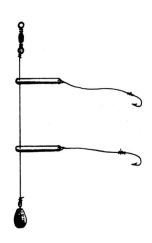

Paternoster tackle is an excellent way of catching a variety of small to medium sea fish. Black and red bream, pouting, whiting, haddock and codling can all be taken on this style of terminal tackle. Many anglers use clear plastic booms in a variety of rigs to keep their hook length clear of the main line. These booms can be obtained from most tackle shops.

A plastic boom paternoster.

Wander Tackle

This rig is designed for catching plaice and large dabs. It is similar to a standard ledger, but instead of the conventional sliding leads it incorporates two spiral leads. A plastic boom is set between these leads and a second hook attached to the end of the main line. This terminal rig is used from a drifting boat, the boom stopping the second hook from tangling.

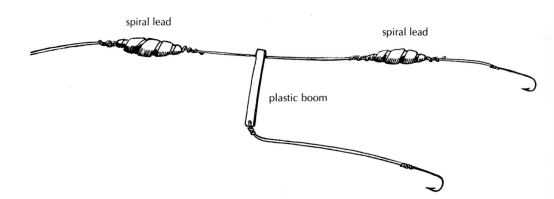

spiral lead

spiral lead

plastic boom

Wander tackle for flat-fish

Orkney-Style Ling Rig

An interesting variant on the paternoster is the Orkney-style ling rig. Made up of a wire or French boom with an attractor spoon and wire trace attached to its end, it attracts ling by its vibration and visual effect.

40

Orcadian anglers use a silver spoon for the attractor blade. This can be so highly effective that an occasional monster halibut is hooked.

Flounder Fishing Rig

Flounder anglers fishing from an anchored or drifting dinghy sometimes use an attractor spoon beneath a float. This rig is designed to keep the spoon and bait working just off the sea bed. The float and spoon tackle can be cast out and wound slowly back to an anchored dinghy. As an alternative, it can be cast out and allowed to work at tide drift speed. Both techniques work well and often successfully catch fish when more conventional methods fail.

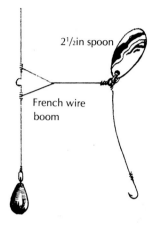

2¹/₂in spoon

French wire boom

Orkney-style ling tackle.

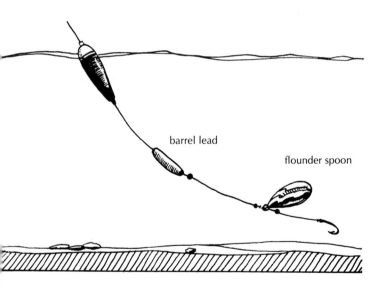

barrel lead

flounder spoon

A flounder fishing rig.

Rig Protection

Rigs are best made up at home and kept in a proper rig wallet ready for use. A good tip is to wrap each individual rig in cling film. This will keep it perfectly tidy at all times.

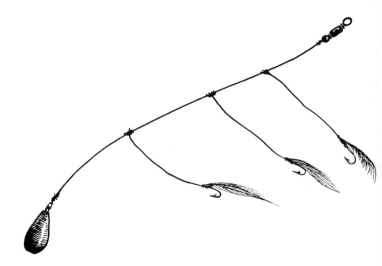

Mackerel feathers.

Mackerel Feathers

When mackerel are in superabundance a set of special mackerel feathers can be deadly. These mackerel feathers were originally made out of the dyed neck feathers of chickens. Such feathers are still available today but are inferior to the more synthetic materials used to make mackerel tackle. The main problem with real feather lures is that they do not survive very long amidst shoals of swimming mackerel.

Artificial feathers are available in sets of four, six, eight and twelve. However, far too many anglers are too eager, operating on the principle that the more feathers there are on a line, the more mackerel they can catch. It is better to buy a set containing six feathers and cut them in half to make two sets of three feathers. These shorter sets are just as efficient and a lot less dangerous than the multi-feather rigs. Six or more loose feathers jiggling about in a crowded boat can inflict some serious injuries. With the totally manageable three-feather rig this danger element is cut to an acceptable minimum. Feathers are worked by raising and lowering the rod tip. Mackerel change feeding levels and have to be searched for – sometimes they are just under the boat, sometimes at midwater or sea-bed level.

42

Anti-Tangle Booms

For ledger fishing in deep water it is essential to use an anti-tangle boom. This can be made of wire or better still semi-stiff plastic tubing. There are some excellent Eddystone lead booms on the market, that are long enough for deepwater fishing. Without these elongated booms, the hook link has a tendency to fly up and wrap round the reel line as the tackle is dropped to the sea bed. Boom tubing can be purchased in most good tackle shops. These tubes can then be cut into 9 or 10in lengths and fitted with a wire connection on which to hang the lead.

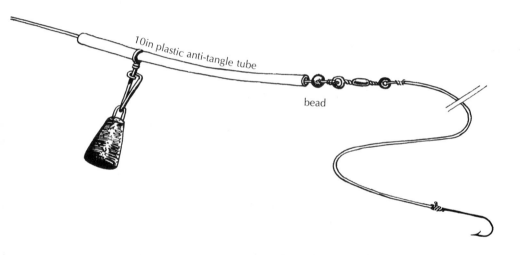

10in plastic anti-tangle tube

bead

By making up your own boom it is possible to save quite a lot of money in the course of a season. Setting up the rig is simple. The reel line passes directly through the plastic boom. A large plastic bead is then slid onto the line and the end of the line knotted to a trace swivel. The trace material and the length of the actual trace depends on the type of fish you expect to catch. For conger, dogfish, bull huss and skate a 20in trace length is ample. For cod and tope a longer trace should be employed.

Using anti-tangle booms can save a lot of time. Such booms have become standard tackle for most top anglers.

A plastic anti-tangle tube.

Boat Fishing

Fresh Fish Bait

One of the most popular baits is a fillet or fish cutting from a fresh mackerel, herring or pouting. To cut a fillet hold the tail of the bait and cut up towards the fish's head. A sharp knife is essential and should be held at a slight angle so that the blade does not cut into the backbone of the fish. Always cut away from yourself. When the bait has been cut almost to the gills the knife should be removed and a single cut used to sever the fillet from the carcass. The bait fish can then be turned over and the process repeated.

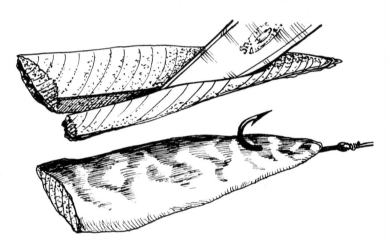

A mackerel fillet cut lengthwise.

Three good baits can be removed – two fillets, and a head and guts. The fillets can be used whole or cut into three or four long strips. To cut these strips lay the fillet skin downwards on the bait board and make the cuts through the flesh into the skin. A bait laid in this way will cut cleanly and not slip on the cutting board.

Squid Baits

Imported calamari squid are widely used for cod bait and are normally sold frozen in 5lb boxes. Locally caught squid and cuttlefish also make good baits but are large and have to be cut for use. Calamari single squid can be used in two ways.

44

The commonest method is to make up a two-hook rig incorporating one large 6–O or 8–O O'Shaugnessy hook and an up-trace bait-holding hook, normally size 2–O. This bait holder has a rubber sleeve on its shank to stop it sliding too easily on the trace. This is simply a support hook which holds the bait in a natural position.

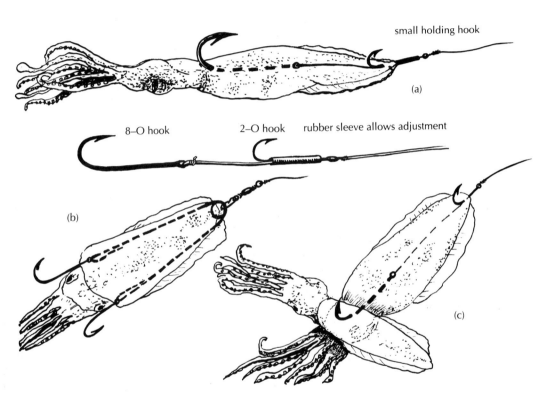

The more complex squid spreader has to be made up at home from sprung steel wire. When depressed, the wire slides easily into the body cavity of calamari squid. Once pressure is released, the spreader expands to grip the squid from the inside out. A very effective big cod bait is a double squid. The lower squid is mounted crosswise on the hook. If a hunting cod takes the first squid it should return for the second.

(a) A simple squid rig, (b) a squid spreader, (c) a double squid hooked the T-method for catching big cod.

Sandeels

A very deadly sea bait is live sandeel. Used mainly for bass and turbot, live eels will attract and catch most species of sea fish. Being delicate little creatures, sandeels require gentle handling otherwise they quickly die. The best way to hook a live eel is through the skin on its back just behind the head. Alternatively, the hook can be passed through the mouth and out of the gill slit before being nicked under the belly skin. Of the two baiting techniques this one gives the firmest hold.

Two methods of hooking a live sandeel.

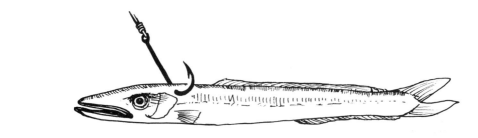

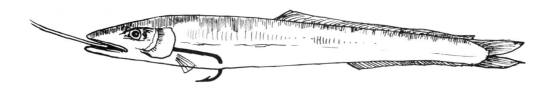

Hermit Crabs

A hermit crab hooked through the back.

Hermit crabs are another deadly but rarely used bait. Large smoothounds are very fond of these soft-tailed little crabs. A good supply can usually be obtained from local trawlers or crab boats. Once de-shelled, hermit crabs should be hooked through the back. Fish rarely have the opportunity to find a hermit crab out of its shell, so when one does appear they are normally quick to take advantage.

46

Cocktail Bait

For some species of fish like plaice and black bream a combination or cocktail bait can be devastating. Strangely, few anglers bother to combine two baits on one hook. A killing combination is a large worm and a strip of white squid. The worm is put on the hook first then the hook point is tipped with the squid. Equally good is a cocktail of worm and hermit-crab tail. When black bream are being finicky these combined baits often induce them to feed.

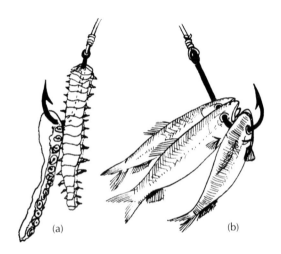

(a)   (b)

(a) A cocktail bait of worm and squid strip, (b) a bunch of eye-hooked sprats.

Sprats

During the autumn and winter months sprats are caught in vast quantities. At these times of the year larger fish may become totally preoccupied with feeding directly on the slow-moving sprat shoals. Large channel whiting love to gorge on sprat, as do cod, conger, ray and even winter tope. The best way to use sprats is in twos and threes, hooking them through the eye sockets. Never try to body-hook a sprat bait. The flesh and skin of these little fish are so soft that once damaged the bait will break up in minutes. Fresh sprats are readily available during the winter months and make a cheap but efficient bait.

47

Boat Fishing

Originally designed for use in the shallow waters along the Essex coast, the uptide method has been refined and adapted for many other areas. In many ways this method can be classed as a major breakthrough in angling techniques. It has certainly proved to be a highly effective way of taking certain species of fish. Skate and ray, flat-fish, tope and bass are taken regularly. Cod, on the other hand, do not seem to respond at all well to a bait presented on uptide tackle.

The Uptide Theory

(a) The lines must be cast up and away from the anchored boat, (b) the lead must have long anchor wires.

The whole concept of uptiding was to get the bait out and away from an anchored boat, because a tide run passing under a boat

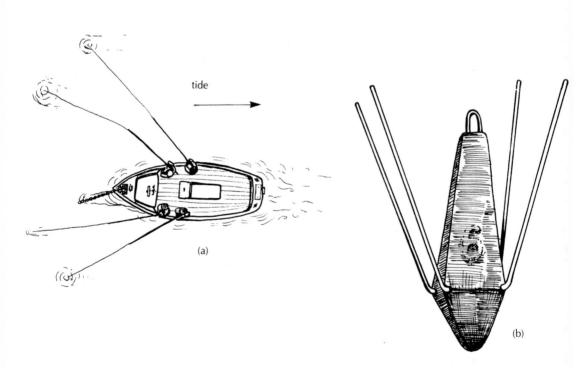

tide

(a)

(b)

keel set up a certain amount of disturbance. Coupled with this, the movement of anglers within the confines of the boat increased the disturbance level dramatically. Fish are known to shy away from this disturbance zone. To counteract the outward movement of fish from an anchored boat, tackle is therefore cast uptide.

Tackle

To fish the uptide method, special two-piece rods have been devised. They are built in two staggered sections – a short butt and a long tip – and are normally $9^1/_2$–10ft in length. Uptiding is usually a light line technique, most anglers using BS line of around 15lb. Probably the most appealing aspect of uptide fishing is this lightness of tackle. A heavy fish hooked on a light line has to be properly played out, which can give the boat angler ample opportunity to get the best out of each fish he catches. Favoured reels for uptide angling are the Shimano Triton Speedmaster and the Abu 7000. When casting with this sort of tackle, a 30 or 40ft shock leader of 30 or 35lb should be employed, which will soak up the impact of the casting.

Safety Precautions

Correct uptide boat-casting is a deadly method of catching fish. Incorrect boat-casting can be just as deadly. To avoid serious accidents there are a few basic rules to adhere to:

1.   The angler using the uptide technique must be an experienced caster.
2.   The lead must be outside the boat when the cast is made, so that it will rise clear of the boat and its occupants.
3.   The uptide casters must stay at the bow end of the boat. This automatically leaves the stern clear for anglers wanting to fish with conventional down-tide boat tackle.

Be considerate. Make sure that when you intend to fish uptide you inform your boat partners *before* you go out. Some anglers simply will not fish in a boat where someone is uptide casting.

BOAT FISHING ────────────────

Terminal Tackle

The whole idea of uptide fishing is to cast the tackle so that it comes to anchor well away from the boat. To achieve this, a special uptide lead should be used. These leads feature long anchor wires which dig instantly into the sea bed. Once a lead is embedded, the line should be tightened gently until the rod tip actually bends downwards to the pull of the lead.

Bites are indicated by the rod tip springing back. This reverse bite indication occurs when a fish takes the bait and dislodges the lead. It in turn gives the biting fish slack line, which encourages it to swallow the bait. Uptide terminal rigs are normally made on the ledger principle. Unlike running ledgers, the leads on uptide rigs are fixed, normally by a 6in length of nylon knotted to the single trace swivel. The trace length is about 3–4ft.

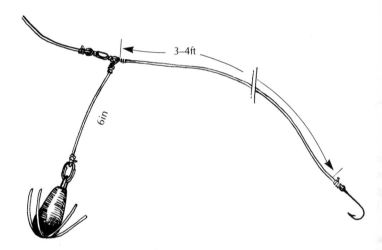

3–4ft

6in

An uptide rig.

Oddly enough, uptide tackle is most effective when used with small hooks and small baits – whole small sandeels on small strips of mackerel being the best baits. These should be used on a size 2-O O'Shaugnessy pattern hook. The exception to the rule are tope, where most of the Essex monsters are caught on a section of silver eel on a size 4-O hook. Large baits do not seem to catch fish.

50

Uptide Fishing

As an aid to casting, the baited hook can be hung on one of the anchor wires. This cuts down wind resistance during the actual cast. Specially designed plastic bait holders can also be used, the idea being that the hook stays in place until the terminal tackle hits the water. The hook is then washed free of the bait holder or anchored wire.

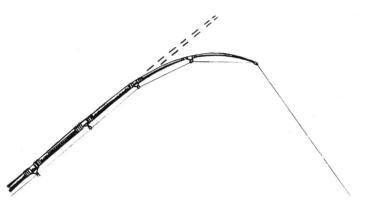

The rod is initially pulled down by the anchored lead, but springs back when the fish pulls the lead out.

Technique

There can be no doubt that uptiding will often succeed when more conventional methods fail. When a good fish is hooked on uptide tackle it cannot be bullied. The technique is to play the fish gently but firmly; if you try to force the fish a breakage is inevitable.

Surprisingly large fish can be landed using this technique. No doubt its popularity will continue to grow with the passing of each fishing year. As more and more anglers experiment with uptide fishing, it is proving its worth, especially in several high tide areas. Such increasingly large numbers of heavy blonde ray are presently being caught that it is on the cards that the next blonde ray record will be taken on uptide tackle. Both the blonde ray and the bass are fish which are harmed by commercial fishing vessels. It may be that when a charter boat anchors in an area, these and other species of fish move out on the path of the boat and its noisy occupants.

51

During the past twenty years improved navigational aids have pin-pointed many wrecks that have since been fished. These have produced mammoth catches of large fish – 100lb-plus conger, monster cod, pollack, coalfish and the odd outlandish angler fish or John Dory. Most of the fishable wrecks are victims of the two World Wars. Lyme Bay has over 200 wrecks. From the western approaches to the Dover Straits there are thousands of wrecks, many of which are still unidentified, lying in water too deep for divers to operate in.

A wreck is little more than a man-made reef. Like a natural reef it provides many species of fish with near-perfect living conditions. In America coastal authorities now create artificial reefs from old motor cars and worn-out car tyres. The car bodies and tyres are wired together and dumped in deep waters. Within the space of two or three years weeds start to grow, shellfish move in and a wide variety of fish and crustaceans make what was once scrap their permanent abode. Wrecked ships follow a similar pattern – whether war or storm damaged, once nature takes over, fish flock to take up residence.

Fish Location

Once a wrecked ship settles on the sea bed, it provides shelter and food to a variety of fish. The perfect wreck is one which

Fish location on a wreck.

P = pollack
L = ling
CR = conger
C = cod

tide flow

P
L
C
CR

settles across the tidal flow. Many naturally sink awkwardly. Even then fish take up a set position governed by the existing tidal flow. Some species live in the wreck, some use its bulk as a shelter, still others live and feed above the wreck proper.

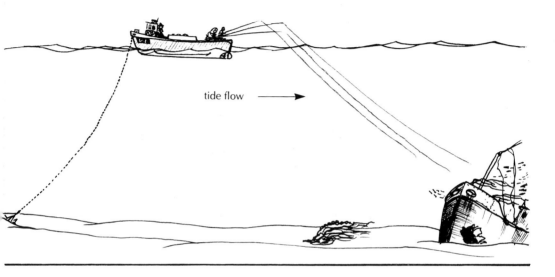

tide flow →

Anchoring on a wreck.

Pollack and large coalfish normally move between the wreck and the midwater mark. These highly active hunters feed on sandeels and herrings swept along with the main tidal flow. Below them lie the ling packs which, although almost conger-like in shape, are strong-swimming fish that like to live just above the wreck. Ling are opportunist feeders happy to take live, dead or nearly dead food. They know that the racy pollack and coalfish cripple and kill many fish which they do not eat, the rejects then sinking down to fall easy prey to any waiting fish shoals. Conger tend to be lurking fish, spending most of their lives deep inside the wreckage, while cod tend to take shelter in the lee of the wreck.

Many charter boat skippers anchor at slack water normally just beyond the wreck, so that tackle can then be dropped back to fish into the main wreck structure. This is important when trying to catch wreck conger, as they have to be hooked and held hard. If they are given a yard or two of slack they will almost certainly snag you.

53

Fish Location at Slack Water

The slackening of the tide dramatically changes the location of wreck fish. Pollack, coalfish and ling move up higher in the water, while cod take up a position directly above the main wreck. The cod, usually lazy fish content to scavenge out of the main push of

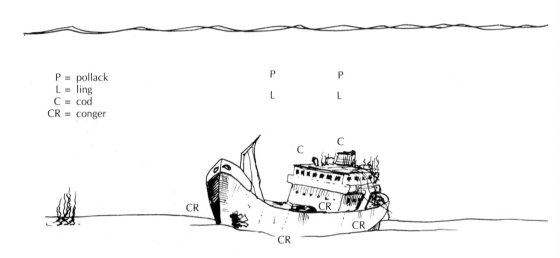

P = pollack
L = ling
C = cod
CR = conger

Fish location at slack water.

the tide, suddenly become active hunters lured by big artificial or natural baits. Conger also tend to make an appearance with the slackened tide. This period can also produce some strange catches, such as large turbot and angler fish which often use a deep wreck as shelter and feed actively at slack water, as well as the John Dory which turns up regularly around wrecks. Most wreck dory are very large for their species.

Tackle

Many anglers use multi baits at slack water, hoping to hook two or three big cod at the same time. However, this is usually more than

54

most sets of tackle can take. Invariably, the tackle will break and fish, being tethered together, will probably fight each other and finally die a sad death harnessed together. By sticking to one or two hooks, you therefore stand a better chance of getting a good catch. If you use more hooks your tackle is liable to be destroyed.

This is a rough tough sport where strong tackle is essential. A 50 or even 80lb-class boat rod is essential. If you try to fish with a lighter rod, you are bound to lose the majority of the fish you hook.

P = pollack
L = ling
C = cod
CR = conger

Movement of Fish as Tide Changes

Movement of fish as tide changes.

When the tide changes and starts to run the other way all fish except conger change sides. While conger simply retire deeper into the wreck, cod are probably the first fish over the wreck. Pollack, coalfish and ling also simply sink down lower in the water. Most wrecks can be fished on both tides. Very occasionally, however, the fish may move to an adjacent wreck, their movements obviously matching those of bait fish.

Wreck fishing is an extremely popular part of the boat fishing scene. Catches are normally large and the fish big. Because most wrecks are sunk in deep water, special booms have to be used to avoid tangles on the way down to the fishing level. Most regular wreck anglers make their own wire booms using coat-hangers or stainless steel wire. Terminal tackle losses are high and to cut costs the cheaper wire should be used.

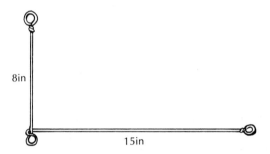

A flying collar wreck boom.

Flying Collar Wreck Boom

This boom is shaped like a long letter L, the longest section (15in) being at the bottom, and the shorter upright section being about 8in long. The boom has an eye twisted into each corner. To make

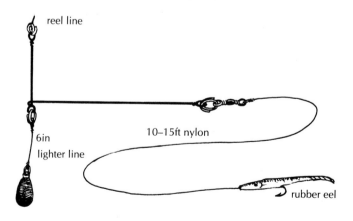

A flying collar rig with artificial lure.

Wreck Fishing Terminal Tackle

t more functional a split ring is added to each eye-piece. The ring at the end of the long section is fitted with a good quality barrel swivel to which the trace can then be directly tied or crimped. The lead is attached to the bottom loop of the short section, normally with 6in of light line or a standard garden tie. Should the lead become jammed in the wreck the line or tie will give, hopefully saving the remainder of the tackle. The reel line can finally be tied to the eye at the top of the boom.

These booms are particularly useful when artificial baits are being used. To fish an artificial eel effectively, a long trace about 10–15ft is essential. Without the long wire boom, the lure would twist back round the reel line on its way to wreck level. This rig therefore helps to cut such tangles to an acceptable minimum.

Fishing an artificial lure on a flying collar rig is a nice clean style of fishing involving no cutting of natural bait. On its day it will take cod, pollack, coalfish and even the toothy ling. The most important thing is to keep the bait and the terminal tackle well apart. Even wreck fish shy away from a fast-moving lead.

Eddystone Boom

As an alternative to the home-made wire boom there is a commercially-made plastic boom designed for wreck fishing. This is the Eddystone boom which is far shorter than the standard wire boom. The Eddystone boom is a neat efficient device but it should not be used with traces above 10ft in length.

OFFSHORE ANGLING _____

Pirk Types

For centuries commercial cod fishermen have used crude lead lures to catch fish. Lead was chosen first for its weight and second because it could quickly be scraped to reveal a shiny silver colour. Although the original lures were crude, they were effective. As time went by this rough type of lure was improved beyond all recognition, and when chrome plating was invented, pirk lures reached their last stage of development.

'Jigs' or 'Rippers'

(a) Do not use a treble hook, as it foul-hooks fish; (b) replace the treble with a large single hook.

Introduced into Great Britain from Scandinavia, pirks were originally called 'jigs' or 'rippers'. A commercial fisherman working a handline did not care where he hooked his fish, hence the name 'ripper'. Even today, commercially-produced pirk baits are still factory fitted with huge treble hooks. Some anglers still

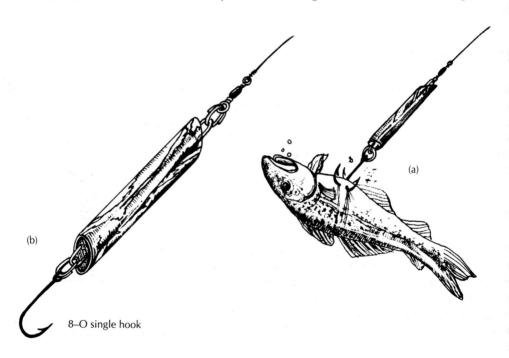

(b)

(a)

8–O single hook

Wreck Fishing Pirks

use these lures, but most replace the treble hook with a large single hook. No true angler wants to foul-hook a fish; by doing away with the treble the incidence of foul-hooking is cut to a minimum. Also, in a contest foul-hooked fish do not count – yet another reason for replacing the giant treble hook. Fortunately, some lure-makers today sell pirks as blanks. The hooking arrangement is then left to the angler to select.

Chrome Lead-Filled Pirks

At its most basic a pirk can be created from a 9in section of chrome lead-filled piping. Disused pram handlebars and old office chairs are often canabilized for pirk-making. Remember, though, that molten lead can be highly dangerous. If you do make pirks, wear goggles, or better still a face shield, and protect your hands with industrial gloves. Home-made pirks have a stiff line loop at either end – one to take a swivel, the other a split ring. A single 8–O hook can then be attached to the ring.

Door-Handle Pirks

Some anglers make their pirks from old van-door handles scrounged from the local scrap-yard. These handles are drilled at either end to take a large split ring. Once armed with hook and swivel they make a light but highly effective pirk. The shape of the door-handle pirk gives it a little more action than the conventional pipe pirk.

Plastic Pirks

There are also some interesting plastic pirks on the market. These are made in two fluorescent sections to hold a range of leads which clip into the pirk body. The two sections are then clipped together and held in place by two tough rubber rings. Another option to make a pirk more attractive is to add a whole squid or a fillet of mackerel. Large cod and the ever-hungry ling love a baited pirk.

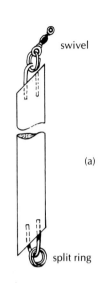

swivel

(a)

split ring

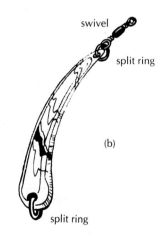

swivel

split ring

(b)

split ring

Pirk types: (a) a chrome lead-filled pirk, (b) a door-handle pirk.

59

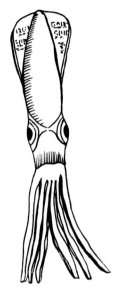

A muppet – a plastic squid in various colours.

Wreck fishing tends to favour the use of artificial lures rather than fresh fish or squid bait, except when catching conger and ling. Pollack, coalfish and cod do not seem to differentiate between natural and artificial bait. In many instances the colour and movement of the artificial lure produce more positive takes than fresh whole or cut fish.

Muppets

One of the most popular artificial lures is the muppet, a plastic squid look-alike which can be obtained in a wide range of colours and sizes. Most tackle shops stock muppets in sizes from 4–10in in length. Generally, the best fish-catching sizes are from 4–6in in length. The larger models are a little too big for the British fishing scene. Designed to look like tiny real squid, a natural food of most predatory fish, muppets certainly seem to have much fish appeal, especially when deep water wreck fishing.

Muppets are too light a bait to work on their own. Most wreck anglers therefore work them above a weight or better still a pirk-style bait. Each muppet is rigged mackerel-feather-style with the hook dangling from the frilled skirt of the bait. Never make the common mistake of trying to use more than two muppets at a time. If you do hook three big fish a breakage is almost inevitable. If big fish are on the move it pays to use just one muppet and a pirk. This will cut down fish losses to an acceptable level.

In deep water a muppet can be made to glow by inserting a 'starlight' chemical light stick into the body cavity. These light sticks can be bought in any good tackle shop and work best when used with lightly coloured muppets – white, pink or orange.

(a) A light stick; (b) using a light stick inside a muppet.

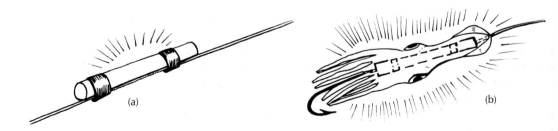

(a)

(b)

Pirks, Muppets and Rubber Eels 1

Although light penetration at the 35–45 fathom mark is non-existent, indicating then that any colour muppet should theoretically suffice, this is far from true. Fish seem to change colour preferences from one day to the next – one day black might be the killing colour, another day red or fluorescent yellow. Because of this it pays to carry a range of made-up muppet traces. If one colour is not having any success, try another until the colour preference of the day is found. A good idea is to use a trace with two different coloured muppets. If most of the fish come to one specific colour, change to two muppets of that colour if you are hoping to hook two fish.

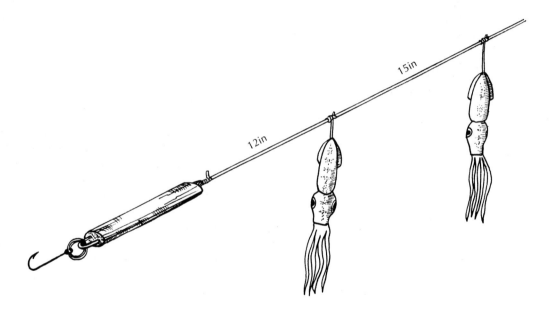

The first muppet should be set 12in above the pirk, the second 15in above that. Hook lengths should not exceed 6in, otherwise tangles are bound to occur. The size of hook depends very much on the size of fish you expect. For general use a size 6–O O'Shaugnessy hook is near perfect. It is strong enough to withstand a hammering from big fish and yet light enough not to interfere with the action of the bait. It can also be hooked to a razor-sharp point.

A pirk and two muppets on droppers.

61

Offshore Angling

Pirks

The size of a pirk depends on the tidal flow. While unbaited pirks are fairly selective fish catchers, fished with bait they can throw up all types of strange fish. One of the commonest takers of baited pirks are big pouting, and if you do not mind catching the odd ling, the pirk hook can be baited with a mackerel fillet or mackerel flapper. Monster wrasse, angler-fish, turbot and John Dory also seem to take a shine to a baited pirk.

Rubber Eels

Not everyone has confidence in muppet-style lures. Many anglers in fact prefer to use rubber or plastic eels. Both the red gill and Eddystone patterns are deadly fish catchers. The colour of eels varies from day to day. When fishing the artificial eel, size of lure is often of vital importance. Do not make the common mistake of believing that big fish prefer big baits. On the contrary, while fish on a virgin wreck may initially hit just about anything that catches their eye, once the wreck has been fished on a regular basis they can become extremely selective. Educated fish will in fact rather pursue the smallest artificial eel they can find. While large eels may look impressive to the angler, they can terrify fish.

Like the muppet, the artificial eel is a lightweight bait needing a pirk or lead to get it down to fish level. Fished on a rig of this type eels can be excellent fish catchers, particularly of big cod, while pollack and coalfish prefer the artificial eel fished on a long-flowing trace.

The successful angler should be prepared to change rigs until he discovers the right combination. Preconceived ideas seldom produce big catches; a variety of rigs must therefore be carried and used. You cannot go wrong by watching others catching fish, taking note of their terminal tackle, then trying to match it. Never be satisfied. Try to think like the fish you hope to catch. Take mental notes of taking depths, speed of lure retrieve and the types of bites you are getting. When you feel a fish biting do not ever stop winding. If anything, increase the speed of retrieve.

A hunting fish expects a live eel to try and escape. If the bait stops moving the fish will take fright and vanish. Pollack can be

Pirks, Muppets and Rubber Eels 2

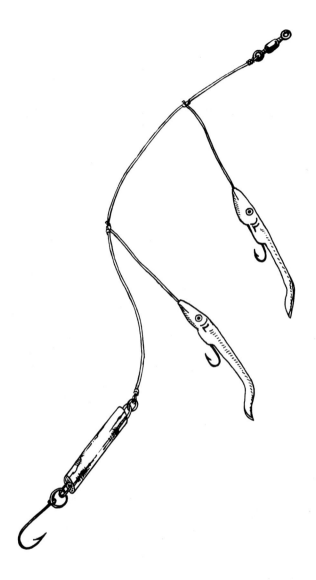

A pirk with rubber eels.

especially finicky biters. Often they will follow an eel gently mouthing at its tail. If you speed up on the retrieve the fish will usually slam into the bait. This induced-take technique can often save a poor day.

Pirk Techniques

Working a pirk and artificial bait is generally a matter of raising and lowering the rod top. This style of wreck fishing is done from a drifting boat. The basic technique is very similar to mackerel fishing. The trick on a wreck is to know where and when to expect fish. Many anglers follow a set routine of lowering the bait until the lead or pirk hits the wreck. Once this is felt they crank up a few yards of line and start to raise and lower the rod tip in a steady rhythm. Although the law of averages says this technique will catch fish, it is invariably the angler who continually changes depths that catches most fish. Try working from wreck level to 50 or 60ft above the wreck. If nothing happens send the tackle back and repeat the process.

A pirk is worked by raising and lowering the rod tip.

If the boat passes across the wreck, the terminal rig will pass through the fish-holding area in seconds. Listen then to all the advice the boat skipper gives. Once the boat is clear of the wreck let the tackle down into the scour, a sort of trench created by tide flow which can often throw up two or three very big cod. If the

___ Pirk, Muppets and Rubber Eels 3

oat drift is set up down the length of the wreck, then practical
shing time is increased enormously. This is fairly rare but it can
ccur.

ackle

ike most anglers wreck fishermen are inclined to carry far too
nuch tackle. Nothing infuriates a skipper more than having his
ecks cluttered up by giant tackle boxes, spare rods and loose
erminal tackle. Better to take just one rod in the 50–80lb class
ange, a working reel and a spare reel. Spare terminal tackle
hould be made up and carried in large sea tackle wallets now
tocked by most major tackle shops. These wallets have been a
nost appropriate invention of the past decade, keeping each rig
afe and tidy in a transparent zip pocket. When not in use, keep
nuppet traces wound up and secured with a strong garden tie.
tow away food and flasks not needed.

Keep your tackle to an acceptable level and you will not
ntagonize your skipper. There is nothing worse than having to
limb over heaps of tackle to gaff or net fish. When it comes
o reel lines for wreck fishing, forget about wire and Dacron lines.
Vire can be dangerous if it has to be broken out by hand and
)acron, once tangled, can end up looking like a cat's cradle.

Nylon lines are the answer. The ideal BS for nylon is 50lb. You
an use 100 or 150lb nylon for traces but not for the reel line. The
eason is simple. A 50lb line can be broken out by hand. If you
iang your terminal tackle into a wreck with an 80 or 100lb BS
ine, it can be almost impossible to break free.

Wreck fishing can be a rugged sport. To take some of the sheer
abour out of this style of angling, it helps to move with the times.
Although the Penn 6–O Senator may have been the wrecking reel
en years ago, compared with the modern titanium reels it is both
ieavy and clumsy. The best reels now available in this country are
vithout question the Shimano TLD20 and 25 models. Holding
olenty of line, these reels are light to use and strong enough to
tand years of hard work.

Drag can be increased or decreased by a simple forwards or
iackwards movement of the lever. This system is ideal for fast-
noving wreck fish like pollack and coalfish.

65

Spinning baits are legion. Ranging from simple metal mackerel spinners to complex plugs and hi-tech spoons, artificial baits are today still in their infancy in the UK. However, in America lure fishing is a well practised art, so much so that most British killing baits have their origin there. Unfortunately, for every good lure there are many that are designed to catch anglers rather than fish. Lure collecting can become a hobby. Unless intentional, beware therefore of accumulating lures in this way. Purchase only those that are proven fish catchers.

Red Gill Eels

Probably the most successful sea fishing lure in Britain is the red gill eel. Originated by the late Alex Ingram of Mevagissey, Cornwall, this is a minor masterpiece which has a fast tail-waggle that few fish can resist. On days when fish are being finicky the red gill eel usually catches more than any other lure. There was a time when a simple rubber eel was good enough to score on any occasion, but fish learn quickly. On a well fished wreck or reef they soon learn to differentiate between an imitation and the real thing. The detail that goes into the make-up of a red gill eel can then make a massive difference.

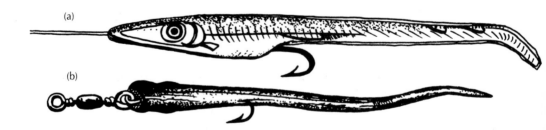

(a)

(b)

(a) A red gill eel, (b) a rubber tube eel.

Red gill eels come in three sizes – large, intermediate or small. Colour may be a critical factor. In deep water, black or red may be the killing colours, while in shallower water, white, blue or silver may be the successful colours. Charter boat skippers usually carry a range of marker pens to change body colours, which can often make or break a day.

Plugs

For shallow-water work, bass plug baits make first-class fish catchers, coming in a range of sizes and weights. Some are designed to float, others to sink at fast or slow speeds. Good plugs are expensive. There are plenty of cheap versions in tackle shops, but most of these are useless. If they do have a good action then the hooks and fittings are of poor quality. Salt water soon finds the weak spots in metal and a cheap plug will start to corrode the moment it hits the surface. Names of plugs to look for are Rebel and Rapala. These can be obtained with a near-perfect mackerel finish that will fool even the most cautious bass. A good pattern with a fine wiggly action is the jointed plug.

(a)

(b)

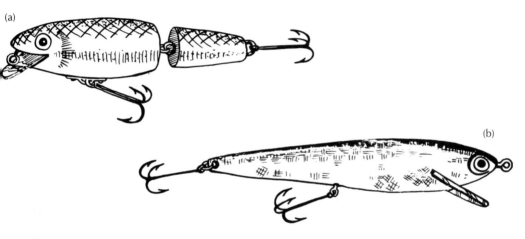

Every plug has a pronounced metal or plastic lip or diving vane which works on rate of retrieve. The faster you wind a plug back, the deeper it will dive. This diving vane also gives the lure its swimming action. Many of today's plugs are so finely 'tuned' that they look just like live fish when used. Some plugs are made in bright fluorescent colours, which may look unnatural in a shop but effectively catch fish. Extra action can be imparted to a plug bait by varying the speed of line retrieve. The rod top can also be turned from side to side, creating a zigzag movement that predators find fascinating. Plugs can be used from a boat or from rock marks and are lethal when bass and pollack are on the move.

Plug types: (a) a jointed plug, (b) a Rapala lure.

Spinners

Spinners also come in a wide range of shapes and patterns, the simplest being the standard mackerel spinner. Bar spoons with a spinner blade that revolves round a central bar are another good fish catcher. The Mepps bar spoon is a particular favourite. Old-fashioned wobbling spoons have now also been brought totally up to date. They come in a wide range of colours and indicate scale patterns. Being large, these spoons look like damaged bait fish, and few predators can pass up the temptation of an easy but substantial meal. Bass are particularly fond of this type of lure.

Types of spinner: (a) a bar spoon, (b) a mackerel spinner, (c) a Toby wobbling spoon.

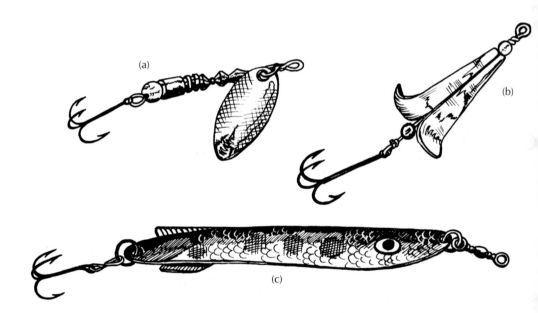

(a)

(b)

(c)

Flounder Spoons

The flounder spoon is a different kind of lure. Used with worm bait it is designed to look like a small flat-fish making off with a good-sized worm. Larger flounders are not adverse to stealing a worm from a smaller fish, so once they see a spoon and

angling worm they invariably give chase and mug what they see
s an easy catch. The technique of flounder fishing with spoon
aits has been around for many years. As a technique it is highly
uccessful, provided that the distance between spoon blade and
ook does not exceed 1¹/₂in. Longer traces just do not seem to
atch fish.

Most flounder spoons are made of white or coloured plastic.
Metal spoons are also on sale, but are basically too heavy for
hore fishing. However, they can be used for flounder fishing from
moving boat. Spin baits certainly catch fish. They are also clean
ɔ use. The rock angler, armed with just a rod, reel and net,
an carry a day's supply of lures in a small box and work on a
oving basis, thoroughly exploring several miles of coastline in
 single day.

1¹/₂in

A plastic flounder spoon.

To fully understand the versatility of the flounder spoon, it is a
ood idea to read *Flat-fish and the Baited Spoon* by the late J.P.
Gallard. Although no longer in print, second-hand copies are
vailable.

Large Spoons

On some West Country estuaries, larger than average flounders
ɔccur. To attract and catch these specimens, local anglers make
poons larger than the usual flounder spoon from copper sheets.

OFFSHORE ANGLING

Since its introduction in the mid-1960s, wire line fishing has firmly established itself. Designed to cut through heavy runs of tide, wire lines now allow anglers to fish areas which would be impossible with nylon or Dacron-style lines. Wire is thinner than nylon but of equivalent breaking strain and, because of its in-built weight, allows the angler to fish with lighter leads. In a tidal situation where 2lb of lead would be required while fishing 40lb BS nylon or Dacron, wire can be fished with just 1lb of lead. Bite detection on wire is much more definite than on nylon or Dacron, having no stretch nor tendency to bow out in the run of tide.

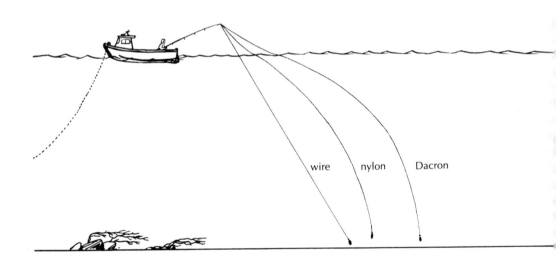

wire   nylon   Dacron

There are distinct differences in the line bow of wire, nylon and Dacron.

Wire line is an expensive commodity. To use it regularly, it is therefore essential to fully understand the types of wire available and their advantages and disadvantages before making a purchase.

Single Strand Stainless Steel Wire

This was the original wire line sold in Britain. Basically a musical string wire, the stainless steel wire gives perfect bite indication at

70

all times. Once on the reel it beds in well, but it has two serious disadvantages:

1. Rust spots. Once these appear the wire must be changed. The lightest rust spot will normally cause the wire to part.

2. Kinks. Single strand stainless steel wire has a tendency to kink when in use. Once a kink is formed, the wire will snap at the lightest jerk or increase of pressure.

Stainless steel wire in perfect condition is excellent, but its tendencies to rust and kink make it a poor buy.

Braided Wire

Thin and extremely supple, this wire lays well on a reel spool and seldom kinks. Unfortunately though, when used repeatedly, the section of wire which passes most regularly through the top rod ing tends to fray. For example, if you normally fish a 95–100ft deep mark, the wire section from 100–120ft will pass most frequently through the top ring. Before long one of the wire strands will fray through, the first indication of damage most probably being when it digs painfully into your thumb. Once braided wire starts to fray, the whole spool will have to be discarded. Despite this built-in problem, the thinness, suppleness and sensitivity of braided wire makes it extremely popular, and it is no more expensive than any other type of wire. Probably the best brand on the market is the American-made seven-strand wire.

Monel Metal Wire

Monel is a composite metal ideally suited to the manufacture of wire line. Thicker than the other two wire types, monel initially feels rather thick and unresponsive. However, its advantages fully outweigh any disadvantages. Apart from not fraying, if it does kink it can be unkinked without major damage. It settles down well on the reel and its initially clumsy feel soon vanishes. Barring careless actions, monel should last one or more seasons and even when scrapped, can be cut into short lengths that make good tope and conger traces.

71

Length of Wire Line

All wire can be purchased in 100m lengths. Like any other line it comes on spools. While 100m is not a practical length for every-day fishing, 200m is ideal. If part of the first 100m does give trouble it can be scrapped and a fresh 100m spool can be twisted onto the existing wire on the reel.

Joining Wire

Both monel and single strand stainless steel wire can have simple loops twisted into them. Braided wire should be crimped using selected metal sleeves. Remember always to twist or crimp a loop that contains a barrel swivel. Terminal tackle can then be hitched instantly to the swivel.

Wire Line Rods

A lot of conflicting ideas have been expressed over the type of rod to use for wire line fishing. Many authors claim that wire can only be used on a rod equipped with a full set of roller rings. This is not true. A full set of roller rings certainly will not harm a line, but it will also not improve its performance. To fish wire properly, all that is needed is a functional top roller ring, that is, a ring that is kept oiled and turns easily. A good single roller will outfish all the double rollers on the market. The best is a single AFTCO roller tip ring. AFTCO rings are not cheap but most effective and, if looked after, will perform well for many years. Rod and wire weight should correspond, that is, a 30lb class rod should be fished with 30lb BS wire, and so on.

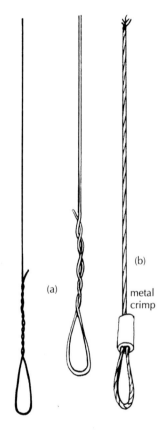

(a)

(b)

metal crimp

(a) Twisted finish to monel on stainless steel wire, (b) metal crimp finish to braided wire.

A wire line must be used with a rod that has a fine running roller end ring.

Reels

When wire line was first introduced, it was thought that a narrow drum reel was the best type to use. The Penn 49M Mariner model was and is still regarded as the perfect wire line reel. However, its gearing is not made for deepwater fishing in very fast tides. It is far better then to use something like a Shimano TLD20 or TLD25. Reels have improved considerably with time, and today reels are lighter in weight. This, combined with new style gearing, make them near-perfect for wire line fishing.

Terminal Tackle

Never attempt to run a lead link directly onto wire line. Instead make up a complete trace that snaps directly onto the swivel at the end of the wire. For example, make a trace from 4ft of 100lb BS nylon joined to a single- or double-hook rig. Attach a snap swivel on one end of the trace and a quality barrel swivel on the other. The sliding lead link is then free to slide between the two

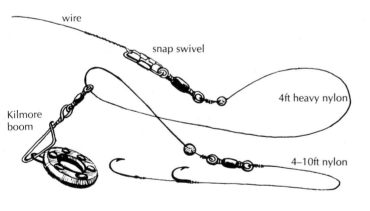

A sliding ledger rig.

swivels. Trace length depends on the type of fish you hope to catch. For cod a long trace is essential, while for skate and ray a 4ft trace may be all that is needed. For fish with cutting teeth, a 12in length of wire can be attached by a swivel to the existing nylon trace.

OFFSHORE ANGLING _____

Wire Line Manners

Not every angler likes to use a wire line. On most boat trips over half the anglers therefore generally use a nylon line throughout the day. Wire is designed to cut through the water. However, nylon has the tendency to bow out. To avoid constant tangles and frayed tempers, the anglers using nylon should fish from the stern end of the boat, while the wire line users should take up a position in the front of the boat. The more buoyant nylon line will stream away down-tide, while the wire line tackle will drop to the sea bed well behind the nylon.

Boat positions must be chosen carefully in order to avoid angry confrontations, especially when they are reversed with the wire line anglers fishing from the stern and the nylon line users fishing from bow end; otherwise, major tangles will occur right through the day. Organize boat positions properly and tangles can be cut to an acceptable minimum.

Trolling with Wire

Bass and to a lesser extent pollack often live and feed in areas of conflicting currents, like the edge of a sandbank or the top of an upthrust reef. To try and fish this sort of area with a nylon line is often a waste of time. Even with large leads the nylon will stream out, taking the artificial lure well away from the hot spot. By using wire and a lighter lead the bait can be fished directly into the most productive section of tide flow, greatly improving your chances of success. Remember that it is impossible to use any form of tackle that has to run on the wire itself.

The best method of rigging a trace for trolling is to use a specially shaped trolling lead which has a swivel at either end. The wire can then be crimped or twisted on to one of these swivels. A strong nylon trace made up of 10ft of 35in BS nylon is tied to the other swivel. A rubber sandeel lure is then tied to the end of the leader, making the rig ready for use. Wire line gives instant bite indication, particularly evident when trolling. Each fish that hits the line slams the rod down hard, so that the fish usually hooks itself solidly in the process.

Wire trolling can be highly productive. Remember, however,

o return small and unwanted fish to the sea to be fished another day.

Safety Precautions

1. If terminal tackle gets caught on a snag, never try to break it free by using your bare hands; the wire will cut easily into your flesh. Use a glove or folded cloth to protect your hands. Never encircle the wire round your hand.
2. Inspect your wire line regularly. If you see a rust spot or sign of fraying, the line must be changed immediately.

A trolling trace.

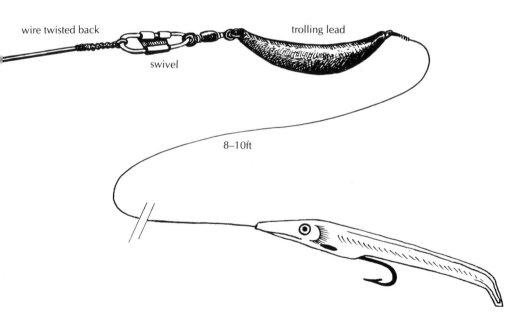

wire twisted back

trolling lead

swivel

8–10ft

A Good Tip

Experience will show that it is better to use a heavier wire, like 40lb BS than a lighter one. Trolling is a rugged style of angling and the heavier wire will stand up better than, for example, 20lb BS wire.

Characteristics of Tope

Once described as the poor man's shark, the tope is a hard-hitting, fast-fighting fish which can provide all the excitement of big shark fishing. Growing to a weight of at least 80lb tope are high on the sea angler's list of desirable fish.

Like all sharks, the female tope grow to a larger size than the males. Interestingly, the female tope hunt on a solitary basis, while the smaller males are very much pack fish, often encountered in large numbers. Normally the females are caught when they come inshore to produce their young. Sometimes these large pregnant females can actually be caught by beach anglers. However, most are taken by boat anglers.

Protection of Tope

So far, the Essex coast has produced most of the really big tope. West Wales originally held the record for this species, but in recent years Welsh tope fishing has declined. Like the giant skate, tope stocks suffered badly from a dramatic overkill by anglers. During the past twenty years the conservation of tope has led to a

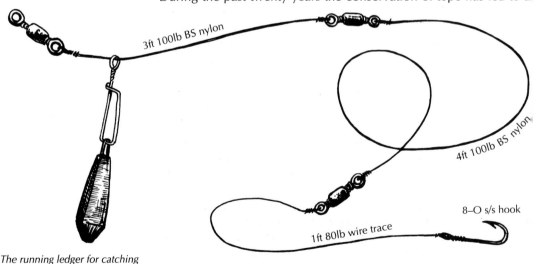

3ft 100lb BS nylon

4ft 100lb BS nylon

8–O s/s hook

1ft 80lb wire trace

The running ledger for catching tope is made up of three sections.

dramatic and welcome increase in tope numbers. Despite this, though, places like the Wash, once famous for tope fishing, have yet to regain their former glory.

Popular Fishing Spots

Off the Isle of Wight vast packs of male tope compete to give a first-class sport. These fish range in weight from 15–50lb, and on a good day catches of over fifty fish are taken. All fish are humanely handled and returned alive, so that tope should be on the increase. Hopefully this situation may long continue. Many anglers go to the south of Ireland for tope-fishing holidays, Lough Swilly, Tralee Bay and Bantry being favoured venues.

Tackle

Tope on the right tackle are tough little sharks well worth any angler's time. By shark standards tope are comparatively small fish, a specimen over 50lb being an exceptional fish. For this reason tope can be caught on standard boat fishing tackle. Most anglers use a 30lb class rod and medium-weight reel. Favoured reels are the Mitchell 624 and the Shimano TLD20. Lines should match the weight of the rod. In shallow water many tope are caught on uptide tackle. However, for the majority of tope-fishing situations a standard boat rod is ideal.

Most regular top anglers use a running ledger rig made up in three sections. The first section consists of 3ft of 100lb BS heavy nylon and holds a sliding lead link stopped at either end by a barrel swivel. The second section is made up of 4ft of 100lb nylon, and the third section of 12in of 80lb plain or nylon-covered wire. Tope have small but very sharp teeth which can cut through ordinary nylon.

Make certain that all your swivels and hooks are the best. Cheap swivels and hooks seldom stand up to the power of a fighting tope. The hook should be an 8–O O'Shaugnessy pattern. The stainless steel O'Shaugnessy pattern hooks are better than the bronze variety which tend to rust. A rusty hook should never be trusted.

Baits

Although tope will chase bait fish to the surface they are normally a bottom-feeding species. They are not fussy and mackerel, herring, pout, whiting, and flat-fish all feature on their menu. However, fish baits must be fresh or live.

Tope will certainly take a cut bait but only when whole fish are scarce. They do not usually expect to find bits of fish on the sea bed, preferring to hunt down and catch their food alive.

Many anglers are convinced that mackerel make the number one tope bait. Statistics would appear to support this theory, but what statistics fail to show is that tope are most prolific (and easy to catch) when mackerel are in superabundance. Try a pouting, small whiting or herring during this same period and these alternative bait fish may well out-fish mackerel. Essex tope anglers in fact prefer a section of fresh or frozen silver eel.

shallow cuts

A hooked whole mackerel with shallow cuts to let the body juices out.

In the end, bait is really what you make of it. Dead or live fish baits are best hooked through the back muscle, well behind the dorsal fin. Although live baits can be deadly, most anglers prefer to fish dead bait, which can be slashed to let the body juices out. This creates a scent lane that can lead a hunting tope directly to the bait.

When to Strike

Premature striking loses more tope than any other angling error. A tope must be given time to take the bait and hook into its mouth. Most tope bites follow a strict pattern. First, the fish picks up the bait and runs off with it. Then it normally stops or slows down while it turns the bait to swallow it head-first. Finally, it moves off for the second time. As it does so, the strike should be made.

The Butt Pad

Like most big fish tope are strong fighters. For this reason a butt pad should be worn and used. Once the rod butt is snugged into the socket on the pad, the angler can apply maximum pressure to the fighting fish.

A butt pad should be worn when catching big fish.

Handling and Releasing Tope

Today, anglers prefer to fish as a sport and return their catch to the water. The best boating technique then is to bring the fish to the surface, so that someone can pick it up by its tail or better still, its tail and dorsal fin. It can then be lifted aboard, unhooked, photographed and returned alive to the sea.

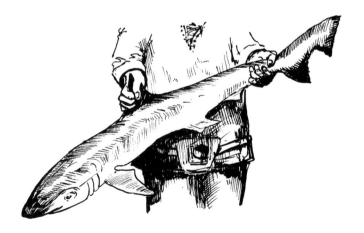

Handling tope.

Giant skate are fascinating fish – huge and old they emerge from the depths like something from prehistoric times. Once common round much of Great Britain and Ireland, stocks of giant skate have suffered greatly at the hands of both anglers and commercial fishermen alike. Fortunately, most anglers today practise conservation and make a point of weighing and then returning each huge skate they catch, following the example set by top charter boat skipper Brian Swinbanks of Tobermory on the Isle of Mull. The result is that common skate are now on the increase in many areas.

What is a Giant Skate?

Basically, any skate which reaches a weight of 100lb or over can be classed as a giant. In years gone by, commercial fishing records show that these fish could top a weight of 250lb; nowadays any skate weighing in excess of 150lb is a monster. Larger fish do exist but are rarely caught by anglers.

Fish Location

Because most of their food is tide-borne, large common skate prefer to take up a position close to the main tide flow, yet out of

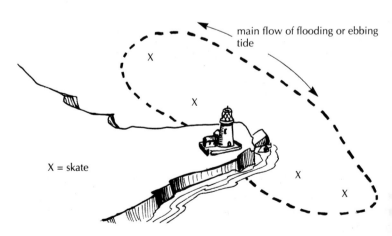

main flow of flooding or ebbing tide

X = skate

A typical skate location is in deep water off a headland.

the main rush of water. A typical position is in deep water off the end of a headland or at the tail end of an island. On a headland mark, the fish will feed irrespective of the tidal flow. The slack area at the end of an island is only productive when the tide passes down the island. When the tide changes, the other end of the island may fish well. However, most islands only fish when the tide creates a slack area around which the main run of tide passes.

Popular Fishing Spots

Most of the large skate reported in the angling press are caught in northern waters such as Orkney, Shetland, and the west coast of Scotland. Strangford Lough in County Down, Northern Ireland, is another skate stronghold. At one time the bays of southern and western Ireland also produced dozens of large skate, but most of these fish were killed, so that they are now rare in these areas. The two top big skate areas in the British Isles are Scapa Flow on mainland Orkney and the rich grounds off the Isle of Mull.

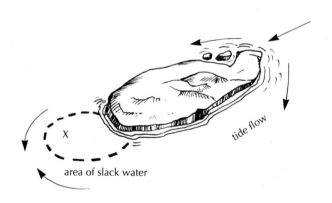

tide flow

X

area of slack water

Skate are also often located at the tail end of an island.

Once played out, these fish are gaffed in the wing, lifted clear of the water, weighed, photographed, and returned to the sea in minutes. They seem to recover well and are often caught again at a later date.

Tackle

Although giant skate do not have the same power as sharks, their sheer wing span and bulk make them a tough proposition. The best sporting tackle combination consists of a 50lb class rod and Shimano TLD 25 reel. This weight outfit is light enough to give the normally sluggish skate a fighting chance, yet powerful enough to stop a really large and determined fish.

Terminal Tackle

Giant skate are entirely bottom feeders, feeding on scallops, crabs, lobsters, flat-fish and any dead fish they find. A plain running ledger therefore makes the best terminal tackle.

Giant skate show no fear of leads, so the actual trace need be no longer than 3ft. Traditionally the trace was always made of plain or nylon-coated wire. Modern skate anglers prefer to use 150lb BS Longliners nylon. Skate do not have teeth but their lips are made up of numerous bony plates. Heavy nylon is capable of resisting both the abrasive and crushing action of these plates. The secondary trace which supports the lead link can be of lighter nylon, 80lb BS being ideal.

A plain running ledger is the best skate rig.

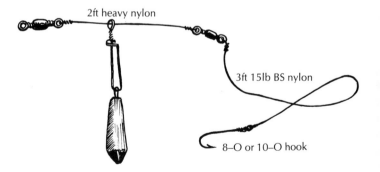

2ft heavy nylon

3ft 15lb BS nylon

8–O or 10–O hook

Even a small common skate has a huge mouth. Hooks must therefore be large and well sharpened. The two most successful patterns are the Mustad O'Shaugnessy and the ultra strong Mustad Seamaster hook. The most useful sizes are 8–O and 10–O.

Baits

In the north the top bait is undoubtedly coalfish; in other areas mackerel are the best fish catchers. Bait fish can be used whole or as fillets, but the most effective is a flapper bait. Flapper baits are created by taking a whole fish and cutting it up from the tail towards the head. When one side is cut, the bait should be turned

A coalfish flapper bait.

over and the process repeated. The revealed backbone complete with tail is then chopped away. This leaves a swallow-tailed bait which is hooked just once through the eye sockets. The resulting 'flapper' bait looks appetizing, and leaves a scent lane of escaping body juices. Skate find this combination highly attractive.

When to Strike

Skate of all sizes gives a false bite when they flop onto an anchored bait. A skate's mouth is situated on the underside of its body, and its eyes on the reverse side. To avoid missing or foulhooking the fish, ignore the first heavy 'knock' and wait for the bite to develop. Once the bait is inside its mouth, the skate usually swims uptide. This will cause the line to slacken. Retrieve the line until the weight of the fish is felt; the hook can then be set solidly. To avoid the fish using its blanket-shaped body as a suction disc, it should be dragged quickly off the bottom.

Be careful when the fish is first exposed to daylight. Always take a back turn on the reel's drag system. If the fish does go down in a hurry, the reel will instantly give line and avoid a sudden breakage.

Conger may be the largest fish many shore and boat anglers may ever encounter. Most of the really large conger or record conger have been specimens caught aboard boats. The shore angler can, however, catch fish 30–40lb in weight.

Characteristics of Conger

As a species, conger are skulkers. Instead of leading a roving existence, they spend most of their life in an idle but watchful state, under overhanging rocks, or around wreckage or man-made stonework. Harbour walls are often alive with conger, especially where discarded bait fish and fish entrails are dumped on a regular basis. Quick to scavenge, conger thrive in this sort of situation.

However, conger are by nature efficient active hunters, more than capable of catching live fish round rocky headlands, sunken reefs and war-torn wrecks. While in shallow water they confine their hunting activities to the night-time, in deep water (where the light never penetrates) these eels hunt at any time. Conger over a 100lb in weight have been caught – under the right circumstances they may reach a weight in excess of 200lb. Such fish, though, are unlikely to be taken on rod and line.

Tackle for Rock, Harbour and Shore Fishing

For rock and harbour fishing a heavy beach caster is the only practical rod to use. Conger are normally hooked in close proximity to snags; a rod therefore has to be powerful enough to pull them out into open water. Let a conger go to ground and you will lose both the eel and your terminal tackle. The sheer physical strength of a large conger will destroy all but the sturdiest of tackle. For this reason shore anglers use a multiplying reel rather than a large-sized fixed spool reel.

The multiplying reel can exert a direct drive on a hooked fish, while with the fixed spool the line has to pass round the wire pickup. Try and stop a good-sized eel with a fixed reel and a serious breakage is almost inevitable. Also, 40 or even 50lb BS nylon is essential.

Conger 1

Tackle for Boat Fishing

Standard equipment for reef or wreck conger is a 50 or 80lb class boat rod with reel and line to match. Remember, terminal tackle losses are high, so the rig should be kept as simple as possible.

A conger trace.

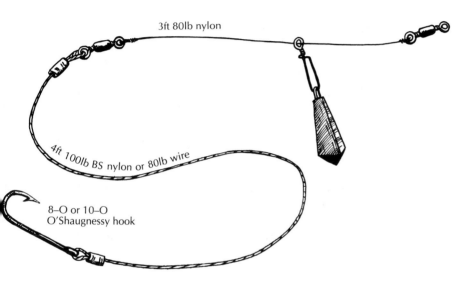

3ft 80lb nylon

4ft 100lb BS nylon or 80lb wire

8–O or 10–O
O'Shaugnessy hook

Conger are confirmed bottom feeders; a simple sliding ledger therefore works for all occasions. The trace is made up of a 3ft length of 50 or 60lb nylon; for shore fishing the trace length can be decreased by 50 per cent. The trace has a swivel at either end and a sliding lead link in between. The terminal tackle consists of a 4ft length of 100lb BS nylon or 80lb BS nylon-covered wire.

The hook should be an 8–O or 10–O flat forged O'Shaugnessy pattern. These strong and easy-to-sharpen hooks are ideal for most big fish other than shark. Never use baitholder hooks; they may look good but the long curved point tends to be brittle. Terminal losses can be reduced by attaching the lead to the sliding link with a garden tie. If the lead does become wedged, the tie will give and the bulk of the trace will be saved.

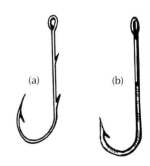

(a)   (b)

(a) Never use long pointed eagle-beak hooks, which are very weak; (b) flat forged hooks are the ideal shape.

85

Useful Extras

Mouth-hooked conger can be unhooked with a home-made gadget called a T-bar. The bend of this bar is simply hooked round the bend of the embedded hook. A hefty shake will usually free the hook. The eel can then be kept or released. Deep-hooked conger are a different proposition. Never put your hand into a live conger's mouth. The eel's teeth may be small but its iron jaw could badly damage your fingers. Rather cut the trace and retrieve the hook later.

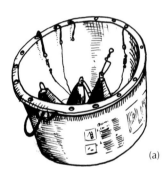

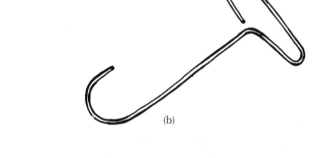

(a)

(b)

Useful objects: (a) a plastic bucket with rim drilled to take traces and lead in bottom, (b) T-bar for unhooking.

Regular conger anglers carry leads and spare traces in a plastic bucket. The rim of the bucket should be drilled to take the hook points, so that they can be carried safely without fear of snagging. All large conger should be gaffed. Make sure, though, that the gaff-head is well secured. As a last resort a fighting conger often goes into a fast spin and if the gaff-head is flimsy or badly attached it will soon disintegrate.

Baits

Conger, like most fish, have food preferences. Being active hunters they like their food fresh. Occasionally they may pick up a stale bait but only when food is scarce. Probably the most successful bait fish are mackerel and freshly killed pouting. However, at a pinch, almost any fish can be used with confidence.

The success of a conger bait often depends on the way it is cut and presented. The best bait is without doubt a fish head with the gills and stomach still attached. To produce such a bait cut the bait fish down behind the gills to a point three-quarters of the way through its body. Then pull the head manually away from the body, leaving gills and guts attached, and pass the hook point through the bait's eye sockets. This gives a firm hook hold, yet allows the head to swing freely on the bend of the hook. Conger normally take a head bait decisively. If a feeding fish tears the dangling stomach away, the bait should be changed immediately. Conger are fussy feeders and will refuse to come to a bait that does not have smell and taste appeal.

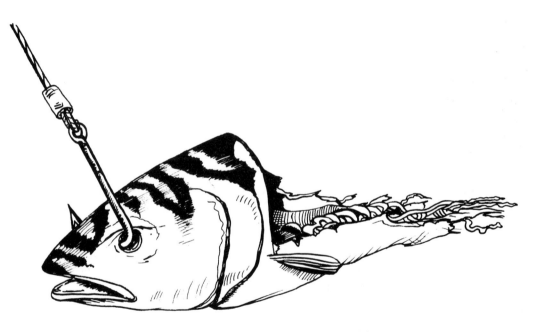

At slack water chopped fish can be thrown out into the fishing area. These pieces should sink rapidly and hopefully act as a form of groundbait.

When boat fishing, a mesh bag or minced fish can be tied to the anchor chain.

A top conger bait is one that is hooked through the eyes and has trailing guts to leave a scent lane.

Types of Shark and their Identification

Four large sharks are found in British waters – the blue shark, the mako, the porbeagle and the thresher shark. The porbeagle and the blue shark are the commonest. The porbeagle has the widest distribution, being found from the Shetland Islands in the north to the Scilly Islands in the south. The thresher shark also has a wide distribution but is a much rarer species. Both the blue shark and the mako are found in the Atlantic Ocean and seldom stray north or east.

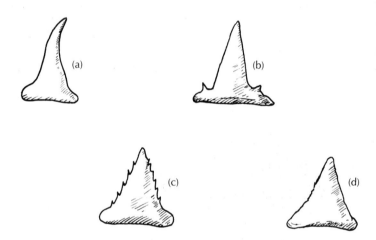

Identification of different shark teeth: (a) mako, (b) porbeagle – note cusps, (c) blue shark – note serrated edge, (d) thresher shark.

The blue shark and the thresher shark have very distinctive outlines which make identification simple. On the other hand, the porbeagle and its near relative the mako are less easy to identify, the simplest way being to examine their teeth. The teeth of a true porbeagle are slim and pointed and have a distinctive cusp on either side of the base. Mako teeth are long and snagged, showing no base cusp.

Feeding Habits

All sharks are dependent on shoal fish as a main source of food. They prey most commonly on shoaling mackerel and herring.

When these fish are in short supply sharks may dive deep to feed on bottom and wreck-living fish.

Baits

All sharks have an acute sense of smell. Once they have smelt something, they will normally follow the scent lane back to its source. Because of this, groundbait, known as rubby-dubby, is an essential part of successful shark fishing. Rubby-dubby consists of minced oily fish, mackerel, herring, horse mackerel and pilchard being the best. Bran and fish oil are also added to help the scent lane spread. This smelly mixture is then tipped into mesh bags and hung over the side of the boat. Most boats use two bags, one on the side where the baits are being fished, the second on the

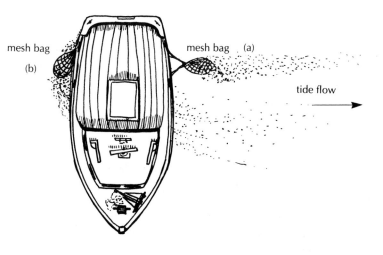

mesh bag
(b)

mesh bag   (a)

tide flow

other side. The first bag releases bait particles into the top layers of water while the second bag sends the bait particles down under the boat keel to lay a substantially deeper trail. In effect, sharks are then attracted from all depths.

(a) The dubby is released into the top layers of the water; (b) the second bag of dubby has to pass under the boat and is then directed downwards.

Tackle

Most sharks, even the sluggish blue shark, are strong fighting fish. For this reason a 50 or 80lb class rod should be used in conjunction with a 6–O or 9–O sized reel.

Penn Senator reels or the magnificent Shimano lever drag reels are the best. Many charter boats that specialize in shark fishing provide all the necessary tackle. The reel must be loaded with nylon line to match the poundage of the rod, that is, a 50lb line on a 50lb class rod, etc. Traces should be constructed from 16ft of galvanized rigging wire, each trace split into two sections and joined by a strong central swivel. The hook should be a 10–O Mustad Seamaster. Hooks should be carefully sharpened before use. A shoulder harness and butt pad are also essential parts of a shark angler's tackle.

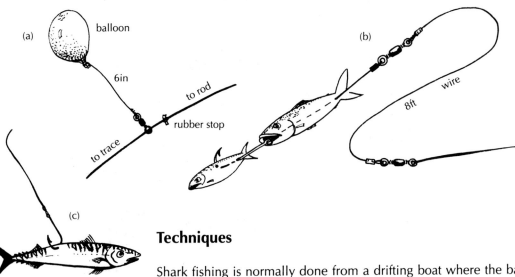

(a) Some anglers hitch a balloon to the reel line with a light thread; (b) hooked dead shark bait; (c) hooked live shark bait.

Techniques

Shark fishing is normally done from a drifting boat where the bait is run in the path of the boat, so that any shark coming up the trail of dubby will automatically sight it. Some anglers use partially in-flated balloons to support the bait at a given depth. Others simply free-line the bait. If a balloon is used it should be inflated to the size of a large orange and hitched to the reel line with light thread, which should snap when a shark takes the bait. Thus the shark will feel little resistance. Too much drag and it will drop the bait and vanish.

The reel should be left out of gear but on ratchet. Never leave the reel in the locked position otherwise the running fish may drag the tackle out of the boat. When a shark takes a bait it normally runs off at speed before stopping to turn and swallow the bait. As it moves off for the second time it can be struck with confidence.

For blue shark, which tend to be on the small size, a single mackerel or similar fish makes a good bait. For the other species a double fish bait is preferable.

Handling and Releasing a Shark

Once a shark has been played out and brought alongside the boat it can be gaffed and dragged into the boat or, if the hook is in the corner of its mouth, the wire can be cut and the fish released.

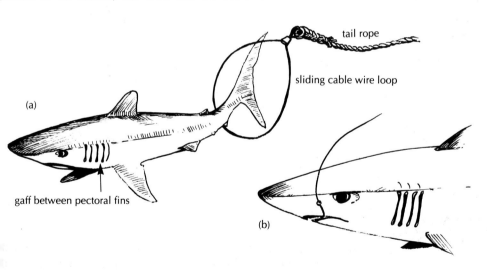

tail rope

sliding cable wire loop

(a)

gaff between pectoral fins

(b)

With a very big shark a wire and rope tailer can be used. The wire loop of the tailer can be slipped over the tail of the fish and drawn tight over the wrist of its tail. A shark should be gaffed between the pectoral fins. This gives a solid hold.

(a) Handling a shark; (b) when releasing a shark, cut as close to the hook as possible.

GLOSSARY

Attractor Spoon   Plastic or metal spoon used above baited hook to attract large fish to bait.

Bait Clip   Used in uptide fishing to aid casting. The trace is doubled back so that hook and bait are hung over the clip. When tackle hits the surface the impact dislodges the hook, allowing the trace to stream out naturally with the tide.

Beads   Used as a stop between swivel and lead boom or in rows as an attraction for flat-fish.

Boat-Casting   To cast away from the boat, using a wired sinker to hold a position on the sea bed.

Butt Pad   Special belt with metal or plastic cup to give support to rod.

Calamari Squid   A type of small imported squid.

Charter Boat   A large boat that takes out groups of anglers on chartered trips.

Crimp   Section of brass or copper tubing used instead of knots or wire trace.

Crimping Tool   Specially designed pliers for crushing metal crimps.

Dacron   Fishing line is made from this man-made thread.

Eddystone Boom   A commercially-made plastic boom for wreck fishing.

Flying Collar Wreck Boom   An L-shaped boom used especially with artificial baits.

French Boom   Wire or plastic paternoster boom used for whiting and other small fish.

Gaff   Strong metal hook used to lift fish into the boat.

Jig   Another name for a pirk.

Lead Link   Sliding boom with clip to hold lead, i.e. Kilmore boom, zip slider, reel boom, etc.

Link/Snap Swivel   As above but with additional clip for fast release.

Glossary

Mackerel Feathers   Brightly dyed feathers tied to hooks, made out mainly of synthetic materials.

Muppet   Common name for an artificial squid lure.

Paternoster   A terminal tackle in which several hooks are carried on short lines attached to the main line above the sinker.

Pirk   Heavy chromed metal bar designed to simulate fish.

Plug   An artificial fish lure available in a range of sizes and weights.

Rocky Beach   Consists of many rock formations surrounded by flat sand or gravel.

Rubby Dubby   Minced fish, bran and fish oil used to attract sharks.

Rubby Dubby Bag   Mesh bag used to hold 'dubby' hung over the side of a boat. This type of bag releases a constant trail of bait particles in the sea.

Shirvy   Groundbait made up of minced fish or meat, fish or animal blood, and bran.

Shoulder Harness   Used as a support when clipped to reel lugs.

Sliding Float   Float designed for use in water deeper than rod length. Fishing depth determined by section of rubber band hitched to the reel line.

Spiral Link   Means of joining trace to line, yet retaining rapid release principle.

Steep to Shingle Beach   Drops rapidly into deep water.

Surf Beach   Shallow beach exposed to prevailing winds.

Swivel   Rotating metal device for joining line or trace to line.

T-Bar   Gadget for unhooking hooks.

Trolling   Fishing with rod and running line and dead bait or with spoon-bait drawn along behind boat.

Wander Tackle   Rig for catching plaice and large dabs, incorporating two spiral leads.

Further Reading

Ball, I., *Sea Fishing Properly Explained* (Paperfront, 1975)

Cacutt, L., *The Colour Library Complete Book of Fishing* (Colour Library Books Ltd, 1988)

Gamnon, C., *Sea Fishing* (Hamlyn, 1969)

Gledhill, B., *The Complete Boat Angler* (The Crowood Press, 1989)

Hamlyn Encyclopedia of Angling (Hamlyn, 1985)

Holden, J., *The Beach Fisherman's Compendium* (The Crowood Press, 1990)

Holden, J., *Shore Fishing* (Faber & Faber Ltd, 1979)

Millman, M. et al, *Boat Fishing* (The Crowood Press, 1985)

Index

INDEX